SUPERNATURAL
HEALING

BOOKS BY SID ROTH

The Incomplete Church

They Thought for Themselves

AVAILABLE FROM DESTINY IMAGE PUBLISHERS

SUPERNATURAL HEALING

Stories
of the
Miraculous

SID ROTH
& LINDA R. JOSEF, Ph.D.

DESTINY IMAGE® PUBLISHERS, INC.
P.O. Box 310, Shippensburg, PA 17257-0310

"Speaking to the Purposes of God for this Generation and for the Generations to Come."

This book and all other Destiny Image, Revival Press, Mercy Place, Fresh Bread, Destiny Image Fiction, and Treasure House books are available at Christian bookstores and distributors worldwide.

For a U.S. bookstore nearest you, call 1-800-722-6774.
For more information on foreign distributors, call 717-532-3040.

Reach us on the Internet: www.destinyimage.com.

ISBN 10: 0-7684-2831-9
ISBN 13: 978-0-7684-2831-5

For Worldwide Distribution, Printed in the U.S.A.

6 7 8 9 10 11 / 15

TABLE OF CONTENTS

INTRODUCTION

The Word of God is replete with miraculous healings and supernatural manifestations that occurred in the lives of those who believed and called upon the name of the Lord.

Prior to His ascension, Jesus left the disciples with one of the most powerful commissions regarding the miraculous—a commission of greater works:

> *"Most assuredly, I say to you, he who believes in Me, the works that I do he will do also; and greater works than these he will do, because I go to My Father. And whatever you ask in My name, that I will do, that the Father may be glorified in the Son. If you ask anything in My name, I will do it"* (John 12:12-14).

It should not surprise us when we learn, that powerful healings, inexplicable by doctors, continue to manifest in the lives of those who dare to believe that through Jesus, all things are possible. In this book, you will read about many of those miraculous encounters and how God is pouring out

His Spirit upon His people. After reading these inspiring, true-life stories of God's miraculous healing power, you will find encouragement to believe for healing for yourself or a loved one.

CHAPTER ONE

THINK HEALING
BY SID ROTH

When I was a brand new Jewish believer in the Messiah over thirty years ago, I was a guest on the Kathryn Kuhlman television show. As a result, she invited me to attend her healing meetings.

What I saw was wonderful—major miracles took place, but in the Bible, I had read that miracles were normal for the first followers of Jesus. I thought all believers walked in this same power. So when she offered to mentor me, I didn't give it a second thought. This was a major mistake that I regret deeply. I did not realize that healing had all but disappeared from the Church.

Two thousand years ago Yeshua (Jesus) entered a synagogue and said, "[You are] making the Word of God of no effect through your tradition" (Mark 7:13). If Jesus went into most churches today, He would say the same thing.

OUR EXPERIENCES MUST COME UP TO THE PROMISE OF GOD

If you reach a Jewish person for the Messiah—a Jewish person who knows nothing about Jesus or the New Testament—and give that individual the Bible to read, without allowing Christians to confuse him or her, there is no way that person will doubt healing. If you later try to tell him or her that Jesus doesn't heal today or that God works in mysterious ways or it's God's will for *you* to be sick to teach you something, then that individual will look at you as if you are mishuggah (crazy). He or she will think you have made the Word of God of no effect by your tradition (see Mark 7:13).

We must bring our experiences up to the promises of God, and not continually water down God's Word to explain our disappointing experiences.

PERSISTENCE IS ONE OF THE GREAT KEYS TO HEALING

As a new believer, I studied under some of the greatest teachers on healing. However, when the devil attacked my wife, Joy, with cancer, we did not experience a miracle. Running out of time, we accepted medical help. Praise God for doctors! God used doctors to save her life, but you can imagine how this undermined our faith.

The testing did not stop with Joy's cancer diagnosis. I was convinced that God wanted me to proclaim healing; so, I would have healing services, but few were healed. One person even died at my meeting! However, I had a great desire in my heart to see people healed. So I persisted. I am convinced that persistence is one of the great keys to healing.

GOD IS INCREASING HIS PRESENCE

God honored my stay-with-it tenacity. First, He started giving me the ability to hear in my spirit that certain conditions were being healed. This is known as a *word of knowledge*. The healings started with necks, then allergies, hearing, and backs. Many were healed. At times, all the people with back problems were healed when I laid hands on them. Even non-believers were healed. Then I started just saying the words without laying hands on people. I found God would heal them just with my spoken word. Lately, He has been healing people without even words of knowledge or the laying on of hands. His healing presence just shows up.

This I know about healing. I am as sure of this as I am that Jesus died for all my sins. Jesus died for all my sicknesses. "Who forgives all your iniquities, who heals all your diseases" (Ps. 103:3).

Isaiah 53, written 700 years before the birth of Jesus, describes a Messiah who would suffer and die for us. Rabbis who studied this passage prior to Jesus coming to earth called this One the Leprous Messiah because the passage says that He was marred and disfigured by our sins and sicknesses. In the Hebrew, it says plainly that He carried all of our pains and sicknesses. "But only our diseases did He bear Himself and our pains he carried....Through His bruises was healing granted to us" (Isa. 53:4a,5b Isaac Leeser translation).

Jesus died for my healing, as well as

for my forgiveness.

In other words, God has done all He will ever do for your healing. It's a done deal. If I never see another miracle I must believe God's Word. "Let God be true but every man a liar" (Rom. 3:4). And "without faith it is impossible to please Him [God]" (Heb. 11:6). I want to devote my life to being a God pleaser.

Where Does Sickness Originate?

Where does sickness originate? It can't come from Heaven. There is no sickness in Heaven. It comes from the devil and demons. "The thief does not come except to steal, and to kill, and to destroy" (John 10:10). Luke 13:16 says, "So ought not this woman, being a daughter of Abraham, whom satan has bound...be loosed." A better Greek translation to English for the word *sickness* is "evil." Sickness is evil. We know there is no evil in God's Kingdom.

Two Kingdoms

Our Messiah taught us to pray, "Your Kingdom come. Your will be done on earth as it is in Heaven" (Matt. 6:10).

The devil tries to get us to use our mouth to speak the opposite. He wants his will done on earth as it is in hell. Both God and the devil need a human to cooperate.

Our faith and trust in speaking and believing God's Word gives God Kingdom rule in our life. Since there is no sickness in Heaven, let's enforce God's Kingdom on earth. Let's not permit the devil's kingdom on earth.

The Greek word for *bind* is a Hebrew idiom meaning "to

forbid" and the word for *loose* is a Hebrew idiom meaning "permit." Here are your King's orders:

"Truly I say to you: whatever you would bind (forbid) upon the earth will already have been bound (forbidden) in heaven with ongoing effect, and whatever you loose (permit) upon the earth will already have been loosed (permitted) in heaven with ongoing effect" (Matt. 18:18, Power New Testament).

UNFORGIVENESS IS A MAJOR BLOCK TO HEALING

Unforgiveness is a major block to healing. Make it a point to forgive everyone who has ever hurt or disappointed you. It's not a feeling, but a command. It's not based on them deserving it. "And whenever you stand praying, if you have anything against anyone, forgive him, that your Father in heaven may also forgive you your trespasses. But if you do not forgive, neither will your Father in heaven forgive your trespasses" (Mark 11:25-26). Let the persons go completely. Release him or her from any obligation to you. When you judge him or her, you are taking God's role. You do not know all the facts. Only God knows the whole truth. When you release the person from your judgments, you become free. Forgiveness does not mean you necessarily trust him or her. Trust is earned, but forgiveness is mandatory.

Guard Your Heart

Always remember, "As [a man] thinks in his heart, so is he" (Prov. 23:7). I am convinced what we feed ourselves is what comes out of our hearts. Guard your heart. Monitor what you see and listen to. Monitor your reading and TV and Internet viewing. Practice Philippians 4:8: "Finally, brethren, whatever things are true, whatever things are noble, whatever things are pure, whatever things are lovely, whatever things are of good report, if there is any virtue and if there is anything praiseworthy—meditate on these things."

Refuse to think about or let anything out of your mouth that does not conform to Philippians 4:8. The devil wants you to curse God when you don't understand. This is what Job's wife urged Job to do (see Job 2:9). Your enemy is never God. He is your best friend and your only help.

To Meditate Means to Mumble Out Loud

God instructed Joshua on the secret of getting His Word from Joshua's mind to his spirit. God told Joshua to meditate on His Word (promises) day and night (see Josh. 1). The Hebrew word for *meditate* means "to mumble out loud." I like to think of *meditate* as God's way to *medicate*. In Exodus

15:26, God refers to Himself as "the Lord who heals you." The Hebrew phrase, "who heals you," is a single word. It means literally, "your doctor."

God says, "For as he thinketh in his heart [spirit], so is he" (Prov. 23:7). Meditating on God's Word doesn't heal you! But meditating on God's Word causes you to believe in your heart, and *believing in your heart* causes your healing to manifest. I also have found reading the Bible out loud changes me! Reading to myself is good, but reading out loud is much better!

Reading the Bible out loud

changes me!

One of the best ways to cause God's Word on healing to manifest in your flesh is to repeat God's Words on healing. When you hear yourself affirming God's Word, you will believe in your heart. When you speak and believe, it will happen!

MIRACLES AND HEALINGS ARE TWO DIFFERENT THINGS

The top healing evangelists of our day have many miracles. I have seen people walk out of wheelchairs totally healed at their meetings. But what about the hundreds of other people in wheelchairs who go home the same way they came? Why are they not healed?

Many times we look for a miracle and miss the *healing*. We plant the truth about healing from God's Word (seed) and believe we are healed (see Mark 11:24). When we do not instantly receive our miracle, we are confused. This then puts us in *unbelief*. Instead, recognize that a *miracle* is an instant healing and a *healing* is a gradual miracle.

The moment you prayed for healing the anointing (power) of God entered your body (see Matt. 8:8). It entered your body whether you felt anything or not. It entered your body whether the symptoms stayed or left. The moment the anointing enters your body, as far as God is concerned, the miracle takes place. But faith must be expressed for your healing to manifest in your body. God has done His part. It is now up to you.

What God Will Do for One, He Will Do for All

God is not confined to formulas. Yeshua (Jesus) healed people in many different ways. I believe that God will use one or more ideas in this book to build your faith for healing and that the healing anointing will splash off the pages as you read these testimonies.

God is not a respecter of persons. What He will do for one, He will do for all. I pray your great passion will be for the Healer, not just for a healing. Become a worshiper of God. Play worship music in your home 24/7, and let your spirit soar to the heavenlies. Make intimacy with Yeshua your great obsession.

Never Give Up

Over the years, I have learned to contend for my own healing and the healing of others. Even if I prayed for 100 deaf people and not one was healed, I never gave up. Today, I see the deaf healed. You do not have three strikes and you are out. You can only strike out if you quit swinging. Keep swinging until you manifest your healing. True biblical faith never gives up. Never give up. Never give up. *Never, never give up!*

After over thirty years of investigating miracles, I do not have all the answers—only God does. But of this I am sure: God is good. God is love. God wants to develop intimacy with you. God wants you to be healed more than you want your healing. Heaven is drawing closer. Miracles are ready to explode on planet Earth!

CHAPTER TWO

GOD'S COVENANT OF PROTECTION— THE 91ST PSALM

PEOPLE WHO HAVE LEARNED TO TRUST THE PROMISES THAT GOD MAKES IN THE 91ST PSALM HAVE RECEIVED MANY MIRACLES AND DRAMATIC HEALINGS. PEGGY JOYCE RUTH HAS LEARNED THAT IF YOU REALLY PUT YOUR TRUST IN GOD'S PROMISES, HE WILL KEEP YOU COMPLETELY SAFE.

Peggy Joyce Ruth is cheerful, warmhearted, and motherly, but she wasn't always such a happy and peaceful person. For eight long years she suffered, tormented by fears and depression until God showed her how to find safety in the 91st Psalm. She says, "I believe that God gave me this answer because I needed to tell others how to be protected from all the horrible things coming on the earth." Here is Peggy Joyce's story in her own words.

A Vivid Dream Changed My Life!

"I used to be a fearful person—frightened of every bad thing that could possibly happen. I had reached a point where fear literally controlled my life. One day, my fears were at such a peak that I did not know how I could go on. I lay down on my bed, and I asked God, 'Is there any way to be protected from all this danger, or do we just have to take what comes?'

"Although my heart posed this question, I didn't actually expect an answer. I was just emotionally exhausted. I fell asleep, and then I had a vivid dream. In my dream, I was standing alone in a huge open field, asking God, 'Is there any way to be protected from the evil coming on this earth, or do we just have to take what comes?' After a few moments, I heard a powerful, authoritative voice say, 'In your day of trouble call on Me, and I will answer.'

"In my dream, I felt so excited that I started leaping for joy. The next thing I knew, many, many other people had appeared, and they were all celebrating and laughing and rejoicing with me over this answer to the question that I had asked. I felt so overjoyed by those words, and long after I awoke, I continued to ponder what it meant.

In your day of trouble call on Me,

and I will answer.

"The next day I overheard someone mention the 91st Psalm. I felt strongly compelled to look it up. My heart leaped when I read in verse 15 the same words that I had heard in my dream.

'In your day of trouble call on Me, and I will answer.' Then I realized that my dream had been sent by God. I knew that the 91st Psalm was exactly the answer for which I had been looking."

IT SEEMED TOO GOOD TO BE TRUE!

"I spent the next six months intensively studying the 91st Psalm. I found that it makes some astonishing promises. It offers a covenant of protection from every kind of harm that can befall a person—sickness, accidents, war, natural disasters—there is nothing that is not covered. If I could believe the words of the Psalm, there was nothing on earth that could harm my family or me.

"It seemed almost too good to be true. My rational mind rejected it. I thought, *This was written more than 2,600 years ago. It does not apply to me. I can't believe this.* However, something inside kept telling me that this was the answer. Then, one day God led me to the Scripture in Romans 3:3-4 that says, 'If some do not believe, will their unbelief nullify the faithfulness of God? May it never be! Rather, let God be found true, though every man be found a liar.' That settled it."

I CHOSE TO BELIEVE, AND I TALKED ABOUT IT WITH OTHERS

"I had to make up my mind that either the Word of God

was trustworthy or it was not. I had to choose. I chose to believe it, but it was a belief I had to work for through careful study of the Bible and meditating on the words. It did not come easily.

"Then I started talking about it with my friends and family members. The more I talked about it, the more I understood and believed it. It is true that faith comes by hearing, even if you are hearing your own voice speak God's Word.

"As I told others about it, I found many who actually put it into practice in their lives. One of these was my brother, Dr. James Crow, who later relied on the 91st Psalm to save his daughter's life."

My Niece Is Healed of Traumatic Brain Damage!

"One morning, my brother's eleven-year-old daughter, Julie, was thrown from a horse. As she fell, the horse kicked her in the head, cracking her skull like an eggshell. It was bad. They sent her immediately from our local hospital to a larger hospital, and when we got there the swelling of her face was so severe that we could not even recognize her. All of her vital signs had dropped, and the doctors could not revive her at first. They told us that her injuries were so serious that she might die at any minute, and that she could not possibly live through the night.

------ · · ● ◆━━━━━━━━◆ ● · · ------

I will not accept your prognosis.

------ · · ● ◆━━━━━━━━◆ ● · · ------

"My brother put his full trust in the 91st Psalm. He told the doctors, 'I will not accept your prognosis. We have a covenant of protection with God. I believe God will heal her.' I think the medical staff thought we were religious nuts. However, as a family we were all in agreement, praying the 91st Psalm for Julie. We said it over and over as we sat in the waiting room, and miraculously, her vital signs came back, but she was still unconscious.

"Her doctor did not seem impressed that her vital signs had improved. He said, 'Even if she does live through the night, she will be brain damaged and suffer severe hearing and sight loss due to the location of the injuries.' He tried to present the facts to us and explained that her optic nerve had been damaged, that the bones in her ears were shattered, and that her brain had severe trauma. It was true that she had been injured beyond recognition.

"However, my brother put his trust in the 91st Psalm, and he refused to let go of his covenant of protection. We all kept confessing that Psalm over Julie, and repeatedly told the medical staff, 'We have a covenant, and she will be OK.' To make a long story short, nine days later she walked out of that hospital with no hearing loss, no loss of eyesight, and no brain damage—totally healed.

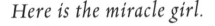

Here is the miracle girl.

"Throughout her recovery, nurses and doctors kept coming to her room saying, 'Here is the miracle girl.' I know my niece would not be normal today, and probably not alive, if my brother had not stood firm on his covenant with God. Today she is a dental assistant for one of the leading dentists in San Antonio, Texas."

PSALM 91: GOD'S COVENANT
OF PROTECTION

He who dwells in the shelter of the Most High
  will abide in the shadow of the Almighty.

I will say to the Lord,
"My refuge and my fortress,
My God, in whom I trust!"

For it is He who delivers you from the snare
  of the trapper,
and from the deadly pestilence.

He will cover you with His pinions,
and under His wings you may seek refuge;
His faithfulness is a shield and bulwark.

You will not be afraid of the terror by night,
Or of the arrow that flies by day;
Of the pestilence that stalks in darkness,
or of the destruction that lays waste at noon.

A thousand may fall at your side,
and ten thousand at your right hand;
but it shall not approach you.

You will only look on with your eyes,
and see the recompense of the wicked.

For you have made the Lord, my refuge,
even the Most High, your dwelling place.

No evil will befall you,
nor will any plague come near your tent.

For He will give His angels charge concerning you,
to guard you in all your ways.

They will bear you up in their hands,
That you do not strike your foot against a
    stone.

You will tread upon the lion and cobra,
the young lion and the serpent you will trample
    down.

Because he has loved Me, therefore I will
    deliver him;
I will set him securely on high, because he has
    known My name.

He will call upon Me, and I will answer
    him;
I will be with him in trouble;
I will rescue him and honor him.

With a long life I will satisfy him,
And let him see My salvation (Psalm 91 NASB).

How to Claim God's Covenant of Protection

"There are promises of protection all through the Bible, but the 91st Psalm is unique in that it is the only place where all of the protection promises are gathered together in one place, creating a covenant or a contract for divine protection. God revealed it to me because I asked Him to show me how to be safe in this world. I believe that He gave me this answer because I needed to tell others how to be protected from all the horrible things coming on the earth."

God's Protection Is Not Automatic!

Peggy Joyce explains that this covenant of protection is not automatic; we have to work for it. "There are things we must do ourselves to obtain protection. As we read the first two verses, we see that we must dwell in the secret place of God, that place of confidence and restful trust. In addition, we must continually say of the Lord, 'He is my refuge and my fortress; my God in Him will I trust' (Ps. 91:2). We must do both of these things to have all the covenant protections.

"We are told in Psalm 91:4 that we may seek refuge under His (God's) wings. The Lord gave me a very vivid picture of what it means to seek refuge under His wings. We live in the country, and one spring our old mother hen hatched a brood of baby chicks. One afternoon when the little chicks were scattered all over the yard, I suddenly saw the shadow of a hawk overhead. Then I noticed something that taught me a lesson I will never forget. That mother hen did not run to those little chicks and jump on top of them to try to cover them with her wings.

Then I noticed something that taught me a lesson I will never forget.

"Instead, she squatted down, spread out her wings, and began to cluck, and those little chicks, from every direction, came running to her to get under those outstretched wings. Then, she pulled her wings down tight, tucking every little chick safely under her. To get to those babies, the hawk would have to go through the mother.

"In the same way, it is under His wings that we may seek refuge—but we have to run to Him. He does not run here and there, trying to cover us. He has made protection available. And when we run to Him in faith, the enemy will have to go through God to get to us. It is important to understand this."

A MOTHER SAVES THE LIFE OF HER CHILD

Peggy Joyce has taught many about our covenant of protection. One young mother was particularly glad she had learned it. "Her four-year-old son, Skylar, went over the side of a cliff after his bicycle got out of control. When his mother found him, he was tangled in the wheel of the bicycle and lying on his stomach with his chin turned around over his shoulder. The situation was so urgent that they could not wait for the ambulance, so the mother and her sister drove him to the nearest hospital. As they drove, they prayed aloud the promises of Psalm 91.

"The local hospital found an obvious break in the C-1 vertebra, so he was immediately airlifted to Cook's Children's Hospital in Fort Worth, Texas. The situation seemed grim.

However, the two sisters never stopped claiming their protection covenant of Psalm 91 as doctors attended the little boy. Finally, the doctor at Cook's Hospital came out of the room with a strange look on his face. He had the X-rays from the first hospital in one hand and the new X-rays that had just been taken in the other hand, and his words were, 'We don't know how to explain this, but we find no head trauma and no C-1 fracture.'

"These two sisters had trusted God completely and believed what He said in Psalm 91: 'No evil will befall you, nor will plague or calamity come near your household' (see Ps. 91:10). Since the day they left the hospital, Skylar has been a perfectly normal, healthy little boy with no side effects whatsoever from the accident."

A Young Woman Escapes From Sexual Assault

"A young friend of ours, Julee, was getting ready for church when someone knocked on her door. As she opened the door, a strange man shoved his way in and attacked her. Remembering that God said in Psalm 91:5,7, 'You shall not be afraid of the terror [what another person can do to harm you] . . . it will not come near you,' Julee started quoting the Word of God to him as her defense.

"It took forty-five minutes of spiritual battle as the man came at her time after time, but her persistence in quoting these words brought confusion and immobility on him—thwarting every attempted attack. During one of those times when he had temporarily lost his focus, she was able to get out the door and escape unharmed.

"Later, after he was apprehended, she found that he had sexually assaulted numerous young women, and she was the only one of his victims who had been able to escape without harm."

You shall not be afraid of the terror [what another person can do to harm you] *... it will not come near you,*

GOD'S PROTECTION COVERS EVEN TORNADOES AND FIRES

Peggy Joyce also illustrates how we can be protected from natural disaster. Her family had a close encounter with destruction when a tornado raged through their community. "We heard on the news that a tornado was headed for our part of town, and when we looked out the window, we could see it off in the distance. A teen club was meeting at our house, and the members watched the tornado, which had touched down and was headed in our direction. The sky was dark and had a peculiar, greenish glow. We could see a large funnel cloud headed straight for our house.

"I'm sure a lot of people were rushing for their storm cellars at that moment, but my husband got us outside, speaking the promises of Psalm 91 directly to the storm as we marched around our house. When we went back inside, the radio announcer was just making the statement, 'It is a miracle! The tornado, which was headed south of the country club, has suddenly disappeared.' God gave us our miracle. Psalm 91 is our covenant we speak in the face of destruction (the category of evil over which man has no control).

"On another occasion the Lord saved our property from fire after relying on the promise in this 91st Psalm.

My husband and our son, Bill, were burning brush in the back pasture of our ranch when an old underground gas well exploded. Fire raced across the field toward other houses. They fought the fire, but it was hopelessly out of control. There was little expectation that a fire truck could get there in time to do any good, but my husband raced off to the house to call them anyway. When he returned from calling the fire truck, to his surprise, the fire was out. One minute it was out of control; the next minute it was out! Jack said, 'Bill, how did you do it?' Remembering our covenant, Bill had called on God, and God had miraculously put the fire out."

God had miraculously put the fire out.

GOD'S PLAN OF PROTECTION COVERS EVERY KIND OF HARM

"In Psalm 91, God lists all the things from which we are

protected, and we can easily see that it covers all of the evils of humankind. It includes all the evils that come through another person, such as robbery, murder, terrorism, or rape. It also includes epidemics and deadly diseases, and all natural disasters such as tornadoes, floods, hurricanes, and other things that man has no control over. Verse seven plainly says, 'A thousand may fall at your side, and ten thousand at your right hand, *but it shall not come near you*' (Ps. 91:7). He even has angels standing by us to help us. This is God's Covenant of Protection."

WHAT YOU CAN DO

Peggy Joyce emphasizes that all contracts have two sides, so we must be careful to do our part. Here is what she teaches people to do:

1. Verse one reveals part of our responsibility: We are to dwell in the shelter of the Most High and abide in the shadow of the Almighty. We are to be like those baby chicks and learn to live under the wings of our Lord. We must root out our doubts and make up our minds to believe that these are not just words for emotional comfort, but real promises to turn things around. You can examine yourself and ask God to help you accept this as the Truth.

2. We must continually tell ourselves and others of this promise of protection as it says in verse 2, "I will say of the Lord, He is my refuge and my fortress" (Ps. 91:2).

3. We must seek God's protection. We can do

this by meditating on each verse and thinking about what it means. For example, as you meditate on verse two, begin to say from your heart, "He is the Lord, the one to whom I will run first. Lord, You are my God in whom I trust. I know you want to be the Source of all my protection; therefore, I will refuse to look at all forms of Plan B."

4. In addition to meditating on Psalm 91, read it out loud. Put your own or someone else's name in it. Thank God for it; thank Him that He loved you enough to make this protection possible. Depend on Him to lead you through.

5. Finally, if there is any point of obedience that He expects out of you, ask Him to show you. The Psalm promises that if we meet the conditions, God will satisfy us with long life.

Peggy Joyce says, "When you pray this Psalm, tell God that you want to know Him intimately, and that you recognize Jesus as the only provision for your life that matters. I promise that if you read it over and over, and if you believe it and say it out loud, then fear will run away from you and you will begin to see real protection."

She sums up: "It is awesome to think that we can be intimate with the Creator and that He will give us a purpose and a destiny. He provides angelic protection and gives us authority over the enemy. Greater power is in the Word of God than any fear or circumstance or situation in your life. Thirty-five years ago, my life changed from despair to victory, not because of anything special about me, but because of the power in God's Word. You can do it too! Go for the gold! It's your time!"

Thirty-five years ago, my life changed from despair to victory . . .

In her classes, Peggy Joyce has taught hundreds on living in God's blanket of protection. Her husband is the senior pastor of Living Word Church in Brownwood, Texas. For adults and youth, she has written instructive books that go into more depth about the 91st Psalm. (See Resources in the back of the book for more information.)

BREAKING DESTRUCTIVE FAMILY PATTERNS

GOD SET LARRY HUCH FREE FROM A LIFE OF DRUG

ADDICTION AND A VIOLENT TEMPER, AND TAUGHT

HIM HOW TO BREAK GENERATIONAL CURSES THAT

HOLD PEOPLE IN BONDAGE. TODAY, HE AND HIS WIFE,

TIZ, PASTOR A DYNAMIC MINISTRY WITH A WORLD-

WIDE TELEVISION OUTREACH.

I f certain diseases like cancer, diabetes, or mental illness run in your family, Larry Huch's message may be for you. Larry has found that when the same problems crop up in several generations of a family, there is often a supernatural power at work that the Bible calls a generational curse. Larry has seen hundreds freed from problems that had plagued their families for generations.

Larry explains: "Just about anything that causes harm or misery can be a curse. Sometimes the same problems pass from one generation to another, affecting even grandchildren and great grandchildren. The key is to look for the same problem repeating in several generations of a family. This familial tendency usually signals a generational curse.

When the same problem repeats in several generations of a family, it may be what the Bible calls a generational curse.

"The good news is that when we enter into a covenant with the Messiah, we have reconciliation with God and the power to break these curses not only from ourselves but also from our children. This is a wonderful truth to know and understand."

Larry has seen the same principles work over and over again to set people free, first in his own life and later among the thousands to whom he has ministered. His own story is an amazing proof of this teaching.

GENERATIONS OF ANGER, VIOLENCE, AND ADDICTION

Born in the inner city of St. Louis, Missouri, Larry Huch experienced turmoil and pain from his earliest days. Larry said, "Generations of anger, violence, and addiction had caught me in their vicious cycles; many generations of my own family were plagued with anger, and the consequence to me was a childhood filled with violence.

"By the time I was nine years old, I realized that to care was to be a victim. I vowed never to cry again, and to be so tough and hard that no one could hurt me. Over the next few years, I became as street smart as I could. I intended to be, and was, dangerous to anyone who tried to mess with me.

"I probably would have stayed on this path, but I happened to be good at football, and that changed my life. I was awarded a football scholarship to college; so I left my old neighborhood and way of life behind.

By the time I was nine years old, I realized that to care was to be a victim.

"In college I was known around campus as a good athlete. The tough life I had left behind made me fearless and aggressive at football, and I was a star player. When you are a star player, everyone wants to be your friend. I *should* have felt successful, but instead, I just felt empty and confused.

"Like many young people, I found that I did not know where I fit, or how to make sense of my life. I started to experiment with drugs, and I got really caught up in the drug culture on campus. It wasn't long before getting drugs started to take over my life."

A DRUG LIFESTYLE

Larry became such a frequent user of drugs that he began to

sell them in order to finance his habit. Once he started selling drugs, he quickly moved up the food chain of drug dealers until he reached the top level. He continues: "At that time, the top level of the cocaine trade was in Medelin, Colombia, so I moved there and started buying drugs from one of the cartels. I hired people (we called them mules) who brought the drugs in to the United States for sale to smaller-scale dealers.

"I made an enormous amount of money from drug dealing. My lifestyle in Colombia was luxurious. I lived in a villa tended by native servants, and had so much money that I kept it stashed in boxes in my house, along with large amounts of cocaine and heroin. When I went out, I usually carried thousands of dollars around with me just for pocket change. There was nothing I couldn't buy."

A Near-Fatal Drug Overdose

Surrounded by drugs, Larry's addiction began spiraling out of control. Larry said, "I found myself getting high as often as ten to twelve times a day. I lost interest in eating; my weight dropped from 215 to 145 pounds, giving me such an emaciated look that my friends were worried, and warned me to slow down."

"I lived for getting high, and then one day I had a chance to die for it. The day it happened, I was alone in my house. I had started drinking tequila early in the morning, and then I shot up a large quantity of pure cocaine to get high, but the cocaine didn't seem to kick in.

I lived for getting high, and then one day I had a chance to die for it.

"I was already so high that I had no idea what I was doing. I wanted that cocaine rush, so I injected myself again. I still couldn't feel the drug, so I did it a third time, and then a fourth. By the time the drugs finally began to hit my system, I had taken a fatal overdose.

"As my body systems began to shut down, I could feel myself losing consciousness. I knew that I was dying, but I realized that despite the reckless way I had been living, I really didn't want to die. Even though I had often told people that I was an atheist, as I lay dying, I just couldn't help calling out to

God. I said to Him, '*God, if you are out there, please don't let me die without finding happiness.*'

"It is hard to describe what happened next, because it happened so suddenly. In an instant everything changed. I knew that I would live, and that I had been saved by the mercy of a God I didn't know anything about."

———— ·· • • ◆━━━━━━━◆ • • ·· ————

I knew that I would live, and that I

had been saved by the mercy of a God

I didn't know anything about.

———— ·· • • ◆━━━━━━━◆ • • ·· ————

GOD, WHERE ARE YOU?

Larry started trying to find this unknown God through taking various drugs and in all sorts of exotic religions, but the experience of God eluded him. He still drifted in the currents of the drug business, but the need to find God continued to increase.

In time, the drug business in Colombia fell apart, and that led Larry back to the United States. He describes what happened: "One day when I was away, thieves broke into my mountaintop villa and stole everything of value. They took my drug stash and all my cash, and there was no hope of getting it back. I just didn't have the heart to try to start over from nothing in Colombia, so I returned to the United States.

That addiction owned me.

"I wanted a total change in lifestyle, so I moved to a farm in rural Missouri and became a vegetarian. I continued to do some small-time dealing to support myself, but my real purpose was to find God.

"I tried hard to get free from drug addiction, but it proved impossible to break the habit. I repeatedly threw my drug needles into the woods, swearing to get clean, but within hours I would be crawling around looking for them so I could get high again. That addiction owned me."

THE PRESENCE OF GOD

Addiction was not Larry's only problem. He also had a violent temper. In one episode, he became so enraged that he nearly killed the man who lived next door to him. Shortly after this, law enforcement got on his trail for drug dealing. Larry knew that he was just one step ahead of the law, and fled to Flagstaff, Arizona. He had been there just a few days when a friend invited him to visit his church. Despite his low opinion of Christian churches, Larry said he would go.

Larry describes what happened next: "I showed up for the service with my appearance revealing my contempt for Christian churches. I was barefoot and wore only a poncho over my bare chest. My hair was loose and hung down to my waist. Tattoos, earrings, and a beard completed my look. My face was gaunt, and needle tracks ran visibly up and down my arms. The church people can be forgiven for being afraid to have me there. To their credit, they did let me sit in the church while they showed a movie called *Gospel Road* about the life of Jesus.

"I was completely unprepared for what happened next. As I watched the movie about Jesus, something began to stir in me. For the first time in my life, I knew I was hearing the truth about God. My heart told me that this Jesus was the one who had saved my life when I was dying in Colombia.

For the first time in my life, I knew I was hearing the truth about God.

"The pastor invited to the front of the church anyone who wished to be led into the life of Jesus. I was drawn forward by a force that I couldn't explain and found myself kneeling at the altar. I knew I had come into the presence of God.

BECOMING A NEW PERSON

"As I prayed, I renounced my old life. I asked Jesus to come into my heart, and to give me a new life. In that moment, I was reborn. A tremendous weight rolled off me. Years of depravity and loneliness dropped away, and I cried for the first time since I was nine years old. I cried for what seemed like hours. For the first time in my life, I felt loved and at peace, and that I had become a completely new person.

I had become a new person with a

totally new chance at life.

"The term *born again* is often used derisively, but it means 'having your spirit come alive and being born into a relationship with the living God.' I had become a new person with a totally new chance at life. It was an indescribable feeling and remains one of the high points of my life."

FREE FROM DRUGS

Later that day, Larry was startled to realize that he had no desire to use drugs. He said, "I was truly high on the Messiah, and felt completely alive. I waited and waited for the drug cravings to come back, but they never did. I had been completely and totally set free.

"That was 28 years ago. Drug addicts go through treatment to get clean and they are taught to think of themselves as recovering addicts. I am not a *recovering* addict. I am an ex-addict. I will never relapse. By the power of God, I became a new person, completely set free from drugs."

After this dramatic experience, Larry committed his life to the Lord's service. He went into training and became a pastor, and had a tremendous compassion for the lost. His church grew quickly, and he became a leader in the Christian community, with invitations to speak coming in from churches all over the world.

STILL ANGRY

Even as his church and reputation grew, however, Larry began to consider leaving the ministry. He said, "Even though God had delivered me completely from drug addiction, I still had to contend with the uncontrollable outbursts of anger that had dogged my life. These outbursts would come up unexpectedly, and when they did, I sometimes went out of control.

There were times when I hit my wife. After violent episodes, I would repent in tears and beg my wife to forgive me.

"Though I would swear to never lose my temper again, sooner or later my control would slip and off I would go. The worst moment of all came one day when I lost my temper and struck my three-year-old son, Luke, sending him flying across the room.

"At that moment it came to me that I had become just like the generations before me, angry and violent. Though I had vowed never to do those things, I had become the very thing that I most hated."

I had become the very thing that

I most hated.

In a moment of revelation, Larry knew that he was

confronting a generational pattern, acting out his anger just as generations of his family had done before him. He went to the Bible and began a study of generational curses that changed his life.

How Generational Curses Work

Larry read in the book of Exodus that the sins of the parents are visited on the third and fourth generation of the children. This means that people can suffer sometimes for things that their great-grandparents did wrong.

Larry said, "The Bible teaches that a curse is a supernatural power that hovers over a person's life, causing certain kinds of problems to occur. It operates like a blessing, only in the opposite direction.

"Generational curses can show up as health problems like diabetes, heart disease, and even cancer, or other disorders like mental illness, incest, eating disorders, and addictions. Circumstances like poverty, family discord, business failures, and divorces also tend to run in families. Genetic disorders are another example of a generational curse.

"The cause of these problems in our lives may be due to

something that our great, great grandparents did, leading us to suffer under negative influences that are not our fault."

Generational curses can show up as health problems...

TRUTH IS THE KEY

Through careful study of the Bible, Larry learned the way to break a generational curse. He explains: "When people learn about the Messiah, they learn that He died to be an atoning sacrifice for our sin. What is often not taught is that when He was put on the cross He also became a *curse in our place* so that we could be totally free. To get free of curses, we must know and apply this truth. The *Messiah became a curse for us so that we do not have to suffer it ourselves.*

"The Messiah taught us, You shall know the truth and *the*

truth that you know and understand shall make you free (see John 8:32).

"Notice, truth by itself does not set you free; *it is knowing and understanding the truth*. We need to *know and understand* that the Messiah became a curse for us when He went to the cross, and that we don't *have to* suffer this way. Then we can go on to apply spiritual principles to enforce our freedom."

Notice, truth by itself does not set you free; *it is knowing and understanding the truth*.

THE POWER OF ACCOUNTABILITY

Larry wrote a book about breaking these curses called *Free At Last.*[1] One important principle that he teaches in this book is that even though the *cause* of the problem is not our fault, our *actions* are our responsibility, and we must repent for them. To get free of curses, people have to take full responsibility for their own actions and reactions, with no blaming and no excuses.

Using himself as an example, Larry explains, "Although the anger pattern came from my dad, it did not excuse me for hitting my wife and child. Blaming my dad wouldn't solve anything.

"For me, it was a relief to simply come before the Lord confessing my sin. It had been such a burden to pretend that I could control my temper. No matter how hard I had tried to fix myself, I had failed to really change.

No matter how hard I had

tried to fix myself, I had failed

to really change.

"I confessed my helplessness to change, and the Lord met me with compassion and forgiveness. The Lord never points a finger to condemn us. Condemnation and accusation come from the devil. God always reaches out His hand in redemption, healing, and deliverance. Our job is to be accountable.

"In cases where we don't really know what our sin is, we can ask the Lord to show us, and then wait on Him to reveal it."

THE PRINCIPLE OF TRANSFORMATION

"As we take responsibility for our actions and our reactions, we usually realize that *we are powerless to really change ourselves*. We can improve our habits, but to really change ourselves is beyond our ability.

"The good news is that God doesn't want us to *fix* ourselves. The Messiah compared that to putting a patch on a worn-out garment. He wants to make us new, to transform us. *His presence in our lives is the cause of change.* God will make your life new and full of new possibilities.

"Just like with my drug addiction, God took my admission of helplessness and began to change me. *Today, I am free of uncontrollable anger. I no longer have to restrain my angry spirit. I am a changed person, and the anger is just gone.*"

THE POWER OF FORGIVENESS

In his book, *Free At Last,* Larry teaches the transforming power of forgiveness to reverse the curse and change it to blessing. In the book he says, "We make a great mistake in blaming our problems on other *people*. Our real enemy is a spiritual power, the devil, who uses people as his tools. The devil has studied methods for destroying people since the beginning of human history. We should be quick to forgive the people who have been used by the devil to harm us, and turn our anger toward the devil himself.

Forgiveness is a powerful

spiritual force.

"When we don't forgive, bitterness mars and ruins our own lives and binds the problem to us, so that the wrong continues to hurt us. As we forgive the people who have wronged us, we release a powerful wave of God's healing in our own lives and begin the path of our own recovery. Forgiveness is a powerful spiritual force.

"The Messiah taught that forgiveness is one of the most important preconditions for answered prayer. He taught us to love our enemies and pray for our adversaries."

FIGHTING WITH SPIRITUAL WEAPONS

"We are free from all curses when we enter into covenant with the Messiah. He took all our curses on Himself when He went to the cross.

"The Messiah taught His followers, 'the truth you know and understand will set you free.' It is important to fight spiritual problems with spiritual weapons. There is no substitute for study and learning what these are. The benefits will come not only to you but to your spouse and your children and your extended family.

Once you break the generational curse, start claiming your freedom.

"Once you break the generational curse, start claiming your freedom. Believe it is yours and make sure your words reflect that belief. Stay obedient to God and let nothing stop you from living in love with other believers.

"Through the power at work within us we can break the hold that generational curses have on our lives, our families, and our communities."

LARRY'S LIFE TODAY

Today Larry and his wife, Tiz, pastor a vibrant and growing church in Dallas, Texas, called New Beginnings Church. Their children are dynamic young men and women of God, active in the ministry and free of the curses that had haunted their family for generations. Larry and Tiz also have an international television show called "New Beginnings." Millions of people worldwide have heard his message. He has authored a guide to breaking generational curses called *Free At Last,* which has helped thousands to change their lives and gain the freedom that Messiah brought us. The following prayer for you was taken from *Free At Last.*

Larry's Prayer to Break the Curse From You

Father God,

I come before You in the name and power of Your son, Jesus.

I admit that I am a sinner, and I ask You to forgive me of all my sins. I know that my life is messed up; I know that You are not pointing a finger to condemn me, but You are reaching out Your hand to help me. Father, as You gave Your Son's life for me, so I give my life to You.

Messiah, I ask You to come into my heart and make me a new person. Change me from the inside out and mold me into who You want me to be.

Right now I break every family curse and every generational curse on my life. I plead the blood of Messiah over my mind, my spirit, and my body. I break every yoke and every bondage from my past, and I sever those ties through the power of the blood of Messiah.

I declare my freedom right now. I claim my liberty right now. I claim all that has been lost to be restored to me right now. Fill me, Lord, with Your love, Your peace, Your joy, and Your victory.

I open my heart now to all you want to do in my life. Thank You for a new beginning. Thank You.

In Messiah's name, Amen.

Now believe that this has been done in your life, just as you asked. Find a fellowship of believers and walk in your freedom.

ENDNOTE

1. Larry Huch, *Free at Last* (New Kensington, PA: Whitaker House, 2004).

CHAPTER FOUR

THE POWER OF GOD'S WORD

EMILY DOTSON WAS NEAR DEATH FROM ACUTE
KIDNEY FAILURE, BUT WHEN SHE FOUND OUT THAT
SHE COULD BE IN SPIRITUAL AGREEMENT ABOUT
HEALING, IT RAISED HER FAITH TO A HIGHER LEVEL
AND SAVED HER LIFE. HERE IS HER STORY IN HER
OWN WORDS.

"Again I say unto you, that if two of you shall agree on earth as touching any thing that they shall ask, it shall be done for them of my Father which is in heaven. For where two or three are gathered together in my name, there am I in the midst of them" (Matt. 18:19-20 KJV).

My Kidneys Had Failed and I Was Just Hours From Death

"I had been suffering from Lupus for many years. Lupus is a terrible disease that causes a lot of pain. The body literally turns against itself and attacks its own organ systems. It is nearly always fatal, but it takes long years of suffering before you die. The doctors had prepared me well, and I knew that my condition would eventually become critical. However, I had survived a number of painful flare-ups, and seemed to be holding my own.

"My husband had not been able to take the stress of my illness, and he had left me. So I was alone in my house one night in January of 1980. On this night, I developed a fever of

103; I had severe pain and was unable to urinate. The doctor had said that Lupus often attacks the kidneys, so I recognized right away that this might be happening. To help myself, I drank two glasses of water every two hours throughout that sleepless night, but my kidneys still did not act. They had completely shut down. By morning, I knew that I was in big trouble.

By morning, I knew that I was in big trouble.

"I phoned my doctor, who told me that I had all the symptoms of uremic poisoning due to kidney failure. I was just hours from death if I did not get to a hospital for kidney dialysis. At first, it seemed like a good idea to rush to the hospital. But then I realized that kidney dialysis would mean going to the hospital to be hooked up for hours to a blood-filtering machine at least three times a week for the rest of my life. It would not help fight the Lupus, and would only delay my inevitable death.

"When I realized that dialysis would keep me alive but would not be able to reverse the kidney failure, I said, 'No thank you. If that's the way it is going to be, I would rather die at home than live like that in a hospital.' I made that decision, believing that I would soon be dead." Emily was not trying to ignore her doctor's advice, but she had decided to quit fighting her disease and accept what was going to happen.

An Authoritative Voice Told Me to Obey Matthew 18:19

"As my pain and uremic poisoning worsened, I weakened and began to drift in and out of consciousness. I knew I was about to die, but I was a Christian. I was not afraid to die if it was my time. I was preparing in my heart to meet the Lord in death when I heard an authoritative voice say to me, 'There is no need for you to die. Obey Matthew 18:19.'

"From years of studying the Bible, I knew this Scripture quite well. It said, where two or more agree as touching anything in my name it will be done for them (see Matt. 18:19). This authoritative voice, which I knew was God, told me that if I would get in a quality agreement with someone, I would not have to die!

There is no need for you to die.

Obey Matthew 18:19!

"I did not have much time before I lost consciousness completely. I picked up the telephone and called a friend from church. I briefly explained, then said, 'Will you agree with me on this, and can you continue to pray? I believe I am going to faint and die any minute.' She agreed, and almost as soon as I put the phone down, I made it to a chair, and I passed out."

I FELT LIKE I WAS SLIDING BACK THROUGH A LONG TUNNEL

"I was unconscious for a long time. Later on, a ringing telephone brought me back to awareness. I had a strange feeling as I awoke; I felt as if I were sliding back through a long tunnel. When I opened my eyes, I was stunned. I felt wonderful! My fever was gone—my pain was gone. Then, I felt an urge to go and urinate, and this was so normal, I rejoiced and was so thankful!

"Imagine rejoicing because you can go to the bathroom! I had placed my trust totally in God, and He had miraculously restored my kidneys! I was not yet healed from Lupus, but my kidneys were normal again. My gratitude and love of God were as overwhelming as the miracle itself."

Although Emily experienced a life-saving miracle, it is important to emphasize the importance of following medical advice when you are under the care of a physician.

EMILY LEARNS THE TRUTH ABOUT SICKNESS AND DISEASE

Over the next three years, Emily continued to battle Lupus symptoms, which included intense pain, weakness, nausea, and difficulty moving. Emily said, "By January of 1983, I was too sick to get out of bed, but I would not go to the hospital. The doctor told me that most of my organ systems were failing, and that I was coming to the end of my life. "

As Emily lay bedfast, close to death, a friend called a Spirit-filled pastor to pray for her. Emily said, "Before he prayed, he explained that sickness came from the devil, and that the work of Jesus on the cross had broken the devil's power. Then he said that if people would believe that truth, they would be set free from disease just as they were from sin. Then he prayed for me, but I felt no anointing or other sensation.

"The pastor had said that I could be free of Lupus! I tried to be polite, because he meant well. I said, 'Pastor, I never heard that before, though I have been in church all my life. Forgive me, but it seems hard to believe this with me lying here sick as a dog at the door of death.'

"The pastor explained that both sin and sickness were works of the devil, and that Jesus had dealt with them both by going to the cross. I asked him, 'What about the medical facts of my case?'

"His answer changed my life. *He said that the medical facts are true, but God's word is a higher truth.* You can choose what you believe, but if you think you are sick, you are believing the devil's lies."

Understanding began to dawn on Emily. She said, "You mean the devil has been making me sick and stealing my joy all these years, just because I let him get away with it, and that I have believed a lie?" Now that she knew the truth, she was starting to get angry at the devil.

She said, "From that moment I started to enforce my right to healing. Weak as I was, I forced myself to reach out and take hold of my fountain pen that lay on the stand beside my bed. I wrote, 'Today, on January 21, 1983, by faith in the word of God, I decree that I am healed of Lupus.'

"That pastor had told me that by speaking the Word of God into my situation, I could change it. I wanted so badly to be well, to be in control of my fate. I was furious that the devil had robbed me of so many good years. I determined to do this, and that nothing but death would stop me from claiming my rights.

"I started speaking the Word of God immediately to my body, and my body began to respond and to gain strength, which in itself amazed the doctors. I began doing this every waking moment. Then I bought a tape set by Norvel Hayes, a Bible teacher from Tennessee, called *How To Live and Not Die*. It was such a blessing. I began to write down every healing scripture I could find, and I faithfully spoke them out loud, all day long.

"I spoke to my body and to the devil and to the disease just like I would talk to a person. I called myself healed when I didn't seem to be healed. I named the body parts by name and told them they were working properly. I spoke out loud to the devil and to the disease and told them to get away from me, that they had no more claim on me."

EMILY HOLDS ON LIKE A BULLDOG

"For 12 months I did this, and the pain got worse and worse. I knew what the devil's game was, however. He wanted to turn up the pain level to distract me from God's promises and make me think it was not working, but I never once gave the devil that satisfaction. He wanted me to observe the lying symptoms of my body more than the Word of God. No matter how bad the pain got, I never once said, 'Oh I am so sick, I'm in pain.' I just kept saying, 'I am healed. By the Word of God I am healed.' Two of my close friends told me later that they thought by me doing this that I had been affected mentally."

Emily said, "Satan repeatedly tried attacking me with doubts. At night, it was the worst. The devil would turn up the pain and attack my mind, saying, 'You're *not* healed. You don't know anyone who has been healed this way.' I realized that these were lies and that they were part of his plan to deceive me. So I fought back by stating God's Word. I knew that if the devil could make me believe his lies, my healing would not manifest. One thing I have learned for sure is that pain is a lying symptom sent from the devil.

"What is real is God's Word. One of my favorite scriptures is the one that says, 'By the stripes of Jesus, we have been healed.' That particular scripture is repeated three times in the Bible, once in Isaiah, once in Matthew 8:17, and once in 1 Peter 2:24."

It Isn't Easy, But It Can Be Done

"In 12 months I was totally healed. No symptom of Lupus was present in my body, and no sign of the disease was evident on any of the numerous medical tests that were performed. The doctors consider Lupus 100 percent fatal, yet here I was, apparently cured. At first they just said, 'You have gone into remission.' However, after six years with no recurrence of any symptoms, my doctor did extensive testing. His diagnosis was that I was truly healed.

"This was 20 years ago. Since learning how to enforce God's Word and use His principles, I have continued to improve in my health. Today, I am in better shape physically at age 75 than I have ever been. I have wonderful joy in living, and I now have the abundant life that Jesus promised in John 10:10. And what I am telling you is that these principles work for everyone. I am healed for only one reason, and that is believing and confessing the promises of God. They worked for me, and they will work for you.

"However, it isn't easy. Don't expect the devil to just roll over and play dead. He has tricks and deceptions to try to make you give up. Don't expect it to be easy, but if you have patience and persistence, you will win. The Word of God never fails."

After she was healed from Lupus, God called Emily into ministry, and she began to develop as a teacher with a healing anointing. People were getting healed when she prayed for them, but she was to have yet another experience fighting for another healing.

Emily Defeats Total Paralysis

Emily describes what happened: "One day I slipped and fell on a slick cement surface and badly injured my back. Doctors did X-ray and MRI studies and told me that the fall had crushed several vertebrae and that I would always be an invalid. There was no hope for surgery. I was paralyzed. I could not even lift my hands. I could not turn myself over in bed. About the only thing that worked on me was my mouth. As I listened to all the medical talk, I knew that the truth was that my health had once again been stolen from me by the devil.

"I was furious. I said, 'Devil, you have made one serious mistake. You have paralyzed my body, but you forgot to shut my mouth. With my confession I am going to drive you out. You are going to regret doing this to me because God will give me a great anointing for healing of back injuries after I get well. Then I will expose how you attack and deceive people!'"

Emily confessed healing scriptures over her body night and day, just as she had done when she fought Lupus. Three months later, Emily, who had been told that she would always be an invalid, started walking, then running and jumping for joy in the Lord. And just as she had promised the devil, she gained a tremendous anointing for healing of back problems.

EMILY'S HEALING MINISTRY

Emily has become a sought-after teacher with a powerful healing anointing, especially for hip and back problems and for diseases such as Lupus and MS. In one example in Alton, Illinois, a little girl of 4 was carried by her mother to Emily for prayer. The little girl had deformed hip sockets, and because of this, her legs were extremely bowed and her knees were turned inward to face each other. The child walked with great pain and difficulty. In addition, she could not run or play, nor could she sleep without pain. Emily prayed for her, and instantly God recreated the child's hip sockets. Now that child is a beautiful 17-year-old, and is a very active gymnast and acrobat; she is full of life and energy.

On another occasion, a 45-year-old lady in Wilson, North Carolina, asked Emily to pray for her deformed left hip socket. Emily placed her hand on the woman's hip, and before she could even pray, she felt movement under her hand. The bones in her hip were reshaping themselves and growing right under her hand.

Praying for miraculous healings like this has become a normal experience for Emily. She has written a book about her experiences and travels widely to teach and pray for the sick.

PAIN, POWER, PATIENCE, AND DECEPTION

Emily teaches that there are two sources of healing. One is by the faith-filled prayer of someone else, and the other is by enforcing your own rights to health as a member of God's family. She thinks the second kind of healing is more durable because you are less likely to lose something you have learned how to fight for and get in the first place.

One thing she wants people to know is that there is no reason to be sick, addicted, or disabled. If people face their doubts and study the Word of God to learn for themselves what is really true, they can enforce their rights to divine health. She says, "Enforcing your rights is not necessarily easy. The devil wants to win and he will fight you with all sorts of lying symptoms and doubts.

"You also must obey the Word of God and act on that truth. God commands us to live without sin and to forgive others who have offended us. In my experience of praying for dozens of people with back pain, only two were not healed instantly. In both of those cases, there was bitterness in the person's heart. When I confronted them about it, they both forgave and were instantly healed. We cannot have both healing and unforgiveness. You should prepare to be patient. The devil is a fighter. He may not give up quickly, but if you are confident, patient, and determined, you will prevail. The promises of God do not fail.

"We must never forget that we have an adversary, and we have to fight to keep satan from taking the great promises of God away from us with his deceptive, lying symptoms. He is a liar, and he cannot tell the truth, but we can trust God. His

Word is sure, and His promises are certain. His Word is an anchor for our soul. It stabilizes our emotions and brings peace to our troubled minds. And if we abide by the words in Psalm 91, we will always be protected, safe and secure.

"God gave me back my life. He restored my energy and youth. I would not be here if it weren't for Him. My life belongs to Him completely, and I won't waste time on anything that doesn't do His work." Today, Emily travels the country teaching others how to successfully release God's power to receive miracles of their own.

How to Put the Power of Agreement to Work for You

Many people have read Matthew 18:19, tried to apply it, and been disappointed when it did not seem to work for them. Here are some ideas for getting a better result:

1. Start by resolving to trust that this promise is true. Root out any thoughts that God's Word cannot be trusted. Jesus said that Heaven and earth would pass away, but His words would never pass away. The Bible also says that God exalts His Word, even above His name! You can rely on God's Word.

2. Superficial words of agreement are usually not enough. The goal is to build a solid spiritual unity with the other person. Spend some time understanding that for which you are going to agree, discerning God's plan for the situation. Seek the Lord's guidance, and listen carefully to the other person's viewpoint.

3. Make sure that what you are agreeing

about is consistent with the written Word of God. Faith works best when you have a specific Scripture to back up that for which you are agreeing.

4. Find the place where the sick person can honestly agree with you. Remember that sick people are often frightened, and may not have the faith level you think they do. You have to find where their confidence actually lies, as well as how God may want to work. For example, if what they can honestly agree on is for their medicine to work or for a planned surgery to be effective, then that is where you start.

5. Once you find your area of agreement, begin to speak it out. Say it to yourself, and talk about it with others. Keep it on your lips until you see it happen.

6. Like everything else in life, if it does not seem to work for you, vary your approach and persist until you get the result you want. We may be dumb sheep who miss it, but God's Word does not fail.

Emily travels around the country teaching others about the power in the Word of God.[1]

ENDNOTE

1.   Emily has published an excellent book about her battle for healing entitled, *From Defeat to Victory.*

CHAPTER FIVE

SURPRISED BY GOD'S LOVE

TO LOOK AT JAN ALDRIDGE TODAY, YOU WOULD HAVE NO IDEA THAT THIS BEAUTIFUL WOMAN WAS BORN WITH A SEVERE DEFORMITY. GOD FIXED IT COMPLETELY WHEN SHE LEAST EXPECTED IT, AND SURPRISED HER WITH HIS LOVE.

Jan Aldridge was born on December 12, 1961, with numerous health problems, including a deformed tongue that was so large that it blocked her mouth and throat, making it difficult for her to breathe and eat. It was such a serious problem that doctors did not expect her to live through her first night of life. Fortunately, God had another plan.

"You Will Live and Not Die"

A nurse named Pearl Whitfield was working near where baby Jan lay in the hospital. She sensed God telling her to go pray for Jan, although she had never done anything like that before. She laid hands on Jan's chest and spoke a Scripture that just seemed to come into her mind, "In the name of Jesus, you shall live and not die, and declare the works of the Lord" (Ps. 118:17). She did this a few times that night. At the end of her shift, Pearl went home and did not see Jan again until many years later.

Against All Odds, Jan Survived

Against all the odds, Jan lived. They found a way to feed

her by holding her upside down, and squirting milk down her throat with an eye dropper. Thanks to the loving care of her mother and father, Jan learned to eat carefully, how to talk, and most of all, how to avoid choking to death.

Against all the odds,

Jan lived.

Jan's problem was more serious than it might seem. She said, "My tongue was so long and heavy that if I opened my mouth, it would tumble out and hang down over my bottom lip. I was extremely sensitive about being around others and always tried to keep my mouth closed. When I tried to talk, it sounded as if a normal person were trying to talk while holding the fingers completely around the tongue. It was stressful to be in school with *normal* kids. In addition, it was difficult to eat. I constantly asked myself why God had done this to me."

If I Had Surgery, I Would Never Again Be Able to Speak

When Jan was 17, an oral surgeon agreed to try to reshape her tongue and make it smaller. This procedure would involve breaking several bones in her face and cutting the middle out of the tongue. The surgeon warned Jan and her parents that it would take seven to nine separate surgeries to accomplish the result. Once they cut her tongue, she would no longer be able to speak.

Jan said, "My parents thought this was too high a price to pay, but all I could think about was that I would look normal! I jumped at the opportunity. I thought like a typical teenager and wanted to look like everyone else, no matter what the price. I begged and begged until my parents finally gave in and agreed that I could have the surgery."

I Found a New Life

The surgery was scheduled, and Jan was looking forward to it. In the meantime, she visited a friend's church. She said, "It turned out to be a life-changing visit. When I first visited my friend Robin's church, I felt that it seemed alive and different from the quieter services I was used to. People were excited about being there. They wanted to sing and pray and praise God because He was real to them.

"One Sunday night, after I had visited there a few times, I suddenly realized in the depths of my soul that Jesus had died for me personally, opening a doorway for me into Heaven. I was profoundly touched and awestruck at that realization.

The peace of God flooded my soul,

and I began to experience the joy

of my salvation.

"The peace of God flooded my soul, and I began to experience the joy of my salvation. I tell people, every chance I get, to press in to that joy of salvation. Once a person lays hold of the fact that his or her name is written in the Book of Life, it is the greatest miracle that can happen.

"I started going regularly to that little Pentecostal church in Holly Navarre, Florida. I realized that Jesus was with me, and that I could live in His presence every day. My problems just were not as important anymore. I still intended to have the surgery on my tongue, and I just knew that things would somehow work out."

THE PASTOR HAS A WORD OF KNOWLEDGE FOR JAN

Two weeks after this salvation experience, Jan went with friends to attend a youth rally at the church of Paul Wetzel in Jay, Florida. She describes what happened next: "The church service started with some singing, but I noticed that Pastor Wetzel had turned away from the audience, and seemed to be praying. Then he stopped the music and began weeping. After a while, I heard him say 'Show me who it is, Lord.'

"Everyone bowed their heads and prayed. I closed my eyes along with everyone else, wondering what was going on. I was amazed when the pastor tapped me gently on the shoulder, and asked me to step out to the hallway.

"He said to me, 'Young lady, I don't know you, and I don't know what your problem is, but the Lord gave me two things to tell you. The first thing is that He loves you. The second thing is that the Lord said to remind you that He will bear your burdens for you. The burden you carry is too heavy for you. The Lord said, 'If I can bear the cross to Calvary, I can bear your burden.'"

YOU CAN TRUST GOD'S WORD

"These gentle words touched me so deeply I began to cry. God had stopped the whole church service with hundreds of people present to give a message to me. I could not help crying, but when I cried I had to open my mouth to breathe and then my tongue came tumbling out. If the pastor was shocked by seeing it, I could not tell. I was too upset to talk, so I wrote out an explanation and told him about the surgery.

"Let's find out what God says about it."

"The pastor said, 'Let's find out what God says about it.' He opened his Bible and read Isaiah 53: Surely He has borne our grief and carried our suffering...by His stripes we are healed (see Isa. 53:4-5)." The pastor showed Jan other Bible verses about healing, and they seemed to leap off the page. She said, "I knew in my heart they were true, and that it is God's will for us to be in health."

WHEN THE OIL TOUCHED ME, I KNEW I WAS HEALED

"After this, the pastor anointed me with oil. When he touched my forehead with just a few drops, the conviction that I was healed flooded my heart. I stood up in front of all those hundreds of people and told them that God had healed my tongue, even though nothing had apparently changed.

"Faith doesn't deny the facts of the situation, but faith believes that God can do the impossible. That was where I was. Tremendous peace had taken me over. And also excitement—I just knew I was healed, and on the way home I started telling people that, but they couldn't see any change."

THEY THOUGHT I WAS IN DENIAL

Jan's parents knew something had happened in the service because Jan no longer wanted the surgery and even met with the surgeon to cancel it. Jan really believed in her heart that God had healed her. Whenever she had the opportunity, she told people that she had been healed, but days, weeks, and months passed with no apparent change in her condition. She remembers, "It was hard to find anyone to encourage me in this belief. However, my family stood by me with prayer and encouragement. More often, I met with pitiful gazes from people who thought I was in denial."

The Bible is full of stories of people who had to wait for God to manifest a promise. I wonder how many of us today just give up too soon.

Today, she says, "Elisha waited for 40 years for the mantle of Elijah to fall to him. The Bible is full of stories of people who had to wait for God to manifest a promise. I wonder how many of us today just give up too soon."

I Had No Expectation
of Anything
Eventful Happening

"I cannot say I ever gave up, but waiting was hard. I was a senior in high school, and senior pictures were coming up. I had thought that surely I would be healed before senior pictures. I guess I was counting on it, but that day, Tuesday, December 4, 1979, came, and I was still the same.

"On that day, and with the way I was feeling, I had no expectations of anything eventful happening. I had been asked to play the piano for a lady who was singing at a Bible study that night, so I did that and then took my seat to listen to the teacher. As usual I kept my mouth closed so no one would know about my problem.

"After a Bible study about angels, the teacher, who had never met me before, asked for people to come up for prayer. The teacher gently took my two hands in her own and spoke a few words about a prayer of agreement. She said that Jesus had taught that whenever two or more are agreed as touching anything, they shall ask the Father and it shall be done for them (see Matt. 18:19). She told me she was touching me, just as it says to do in Matthew 18:19."

My Tongue Began to Vibrate and Burn

"So far, so good. I was more than ready to be in a prayer of agreement about my healing. Then the teacher prayed for my future. As she was uttering these words, my tongue began to vibrate and become warm.

"It vibrated and quivered more and more intensely, but for a while I was able to contain it in my mouth. Then it began to burn. It burned hotter and hotter as if it had been touched with a hot coal. The pain became intense, and I could no longer keep my tongue in my mouth.

"Tonight is your night," she said.

"The teacher left me and went to pray for others. When she was finished praying for others, she was about to dismiss the meeting. She did not seem concerned about my situation.

I was so upset that I had to speak up. No way was she going to leave me in this condition. What if it didn't go away?

"'My tongue! What about my tongue?' I said to the teacher. The teacher came over to me and smiled and looked into my eyes. 'Tonight is your night,' she said. 'You and the promise of God have finally caught up. Now lift up your hands in praise.'"

I Lifted My Hands in Praise

"At that moment, I was feeling a lot of things, but praising God was not on the list. Nonetheless, I lifted up my hands in obedience. To do this, I had to let go of my tongue, which I had been trying to hold still. I realize now that I was symbolically letting go of a lot of things when I raised my hands.

"For a long time I just stood there with my hands in the air. Nothing happened. Then I felt it move a little. At first, I thought it was just the kind of movement you might get from standing still for a long time. Then I felt it again, and again after that. My tongue was getting shorter and smaller!"

My Tongue Was Completely Normal!

"After about ten minutes, my tongue was completely normal. It was small and fit perfectly inside my mouth. I was so filled with joy that I didn't know whether to cry or to faint or to laugh.

For the first time in my life I called

her without sounding impaired.

"I couldn't wait to get home to share the news with my family. The whole way home I practiced saying, 'Mama,' so that it would sound perfect to her ears. I ran in the house and cried out 'Mama!' For the first time in my life I called her without sounding impaired. She and my daddy had been in bed sleeping, but when I burst into the quiet house and called her name, she knew at once that I had been healed."

GOD CARES FOR YOU JUST AS HE CARES FOR ME

In reflecting on the experience, Jan said, "I tried to put

God in a box, to make Him fit my expectations. He is so much more than we can imagine. He is a personal God. He called out to me personally. He is real, and He cares for you just like He cares for me."

As news of her miraculous healing spread, many churches asked Jan to come and share her story. One night, while speaking at a small church in Florida, Jan noticed an older lady in the congregation begin to weep and praise God. After the meeting, the pastor brought the lady to Jan for an introduction.

She was Pearl Whitfield, the nurse who had prayed for Jan that first night of her life, and had not seen her since. She told Jan how it had all happened, and wept as she said, "I prayed that you would live and declare the works of the Lord. And now I see you, after 17 years, standing tall and beautiful, declaring the mighty works of the Lord."

What You Can Do

Today Jan travels all over the country to bring encouragement to those fighting battles of faith. From her experience, we can take these helpful suggestions:

1. "God did not call me to preach because of the miracle that I experienced. God appointed me to preach His word before I was born, and the enemy attacked me where it would do the most harm.

2. "God wants to heal the whole person—body, soul, and spirit—so that the Lord will find faith in the earth when He comes again. Faith is the most powerful force in the universe. Nothing can stand against it, except our own unbelief. This means our biggest battles are right between our own two ears.

3. "We sometimes have to wrestle to get faith for a given situation, but once we do, we must watch our words. The Bible says that we are snared by our words.

4. "Don't be afraid to believe the Bible. We are ready and quick to believe any bad news we hear. Train yourself to believe the Word of God. He cannot lie."

Jan teaches that if people believe in their hearts and confess with their mouths, there is no promise that God will withhold from them. She encourages people to exercise their patience to receive the promises of God. She says, "God is so good. What He did for me, He wants to do for any who will trust Him."[1]

ENDNOTE

1. A CD with more details is available through Jan's ministry. Visit www.JanAldridge.org.

CHAPTER SIX

PASSOVER FULFILLED

DR. JOHN MILLER IS A CHIROPRACTOR WHO WAS LED TO STUDY THE PASSOVER CONNECTION WITH THE LORD'S SUPPER AND THE ANCIENT PROPHECIES ABOUT A SIN-BEARING MESSIAH. BY UNCOVERING THESE JEWISH ROOTS, JOHN BELIEVES HE HAS FOUND A REMARKABLE PATHWAY TO HEALING.

THE LORD'S SUPPER CONTAINS A KEY TO HEALING

John was searching for biblical keys to healing when he came upon this verse, written by the apostle Paul: "For he who eats and drinks in an unworthy manner eats and drinks [damnation] to himself, not discerning the Lord's body. For this [reason] many are weak and sick among you, and many sleep" (1 Cor. 11:29-30).

John said, "This Scripture plainly says that failing to discern the body of the Lord will make you weak, or sick, or cause you to die prematurely. From this, it follows that proper discernment or understanding will bring you healing. Although the Scripture says this so definitely, I had been in Church all my life, and not only had I never heard this taught, I had never seen it applied." John's research led him to study the Jewish feast of Passover, as Jesus commemorated it in the Lord's Supper.

THE LORD'S SUPPER OCCURRED IN A PASSOVER SEDER

The Gospel of Luke describes how the Lord's Supper came to be created. In the following passage, Jesus is speaking:

"'I have looked forward to this hour with deep longing, anxious to eat this Passover meal with you....' Then He took a loaf of bread; And when He had thanked God for it, He broke it apart and gave it to them, saying, 'This is my body, given for you. Eat it in remembrance of me.'

"After supper He gave them another glass of wine, saying, 'This wine is the token of God's new agreement to save you— an agreement sealed with the blood I shall pour out to purchase back your souls'" (Luke 22:14-20 TLB).

PASSOVER WAS A SACRED JEWISH OBSERVANCE

John believes that it is not a coincidence that the Messiah gave this new observance during Passover. He explains: "Jesus came as the Messiah to the Jewish people, and fulfilled hundreds of Jewish prophecies and symbols. Passover was one of the most sacred of all Jewish observances, and literally foreshadowed the deliverance that would come to people when the Messiah appeared.

"Passover occurred at the culmination of the ten plagues that were brought on Egypt, so that the Jewish people could come out of slavery to serve God. Jewish families killed and cooked a lamb, and then put the blood of the lamb on the doorposts of their houses. Seeing the blood, the angel of death literally passed over their homes. The Feast of Passover, still practiced by observant Jews today, commemorates this event."

The Body of the Passover Lamb Symbolized Healing

"The blood of the lamb was important. It was on the doorpost to save their lives—but they were also commanded to eat all the body of the Passover lamb. The body of the lamb was to save their bodies. The Bible said they came out without one feeble one among them. Eating the body of the Passover lamb was the reason that none was feeble.

"There is a spiritual significance here. If we take the Passover lamb as a symbol for the coming Messiah, we can easily recognize that the brain of the lamb symbolized the mind of the Messiah. The lamb's eyes signified the ability to see things the way God sees. The heart of the lamb is meant to have the compassionate heart of the Messiah.

"So, one way of recognizing the body of the Lord, our Passover Lamb, is to meditate on all the parts of the Passover lamb as we eat the bread of the Lord's Supper. One of my friends did this, and his peripheral vision was immediately healed."

———··●●◆————————◆●··●——

Passover occurred at the

culmination of the ten plagues that

were brought on Egypt, so that the

Jewish people could come out of

slavery to serve God.

———··●●◆————————◆●··●——

THE LORD'S SUPPER RESTORED HIS PERIPHERAL VISION

"My friend raced cars for a living, and he had a bad crash. He really was blessed to be alive. However, this wreck had cost him his peripheral vision, which is a pretty severe limitation for a professional driver. One night he was visiting at my house, and as we talked, I explained the power and purpose of the Lord's Supper to him.

"It was about two o'clock in the morning when we decided to share the Lord's Supper together and meditate on its healing properties. I broke the bread and handed him a piece. We took pieces of broken bread, chewed them slowly, and meditated for quite a while on what it meant for Jesus to give His body to be broken for us.

* * *

When he imagined eating the lamb's eyes, his own eyes were healed and his peripheral vision returned.

* * *

"As my friend meditated on the truth of healing through Jesus, he imagined eating every part of the Passover lamb, just as the ancient Hebrews were commanded to do. When he imagined eating the lamb's eyes, his own eyes were healed and his peripheral vision returned."

A Pastor Was Healed of Cancer After Taking the Lord's Supper

"Discerning the body means eating the bread of the Lord's Supper thoughtfully and meditatively, considering all the implications of the suffering that the Lord endured on our behalf. Jesus took on Himself the sins and sicknesses of us all. We meditate on what it means to be free of all that. When we take the Lord's Supper, however, this won't do us much good unless we believe it. We cannot be forgiven for our sins unless we receive it, and we cannot be healed of our sicknesses unless we believe it.

"Many people are healed once they understand and believe this. For example, Troy Miller, no relation, is a pastor in Florida who had cancer of the kidney. He was bedfast in the hospital, not expected to recover. The Lord spoke to his mother, telling her to take the Communion elements of bread and wine to him in the hospital. When Troy received Communion, or the Lord's Supper, the cancer began to disappear from his body, even as he lay there in the hospital."

Another example is from a young mother named Jane who was hospitalized with numerous injuries after a terrible car wreck. The doctors were predicting the worst, but when her father brought Communion to her in the hospital, she immediately began to get better.

HEALING IS OFTEN GRADUAL, NOT SUDDEN AND SPECTACULAR

One thing that Sid Roth often emphasizes is the difference between healing and miracles. He teaches: "Many times people are expecting their healing to take place dramatically and immediately. I think they get miracles and healing mixed up. Miracles are immediate and often spectacular. However, in practice, most healing takes place gradually. By recognizing the value of gradual healing, we can increase our faith immensely. It gives us the patience and confidence to wait on the healing to manifest, recognizing small, positive changes as we make daily observance of the Lord's Supper."

She had been in medical care, but it was giving her no hope.

John describes two of his experiences with gradual healing

through the Lord's Supper: "One young lady was brought to me who was dying from Epstein Barr virus. The virus had destroyed 39 percent of her liver, and she was very ill. She had been in medical care, but it was giving her no hope. At my suggestion, she began taking Communion three times a day, discerning the Lord's body, broken so that she might have her healing. Within two weeks, I received a call from her father who said that her lab tests were starting to come back as normal. A year later, she was in perfect health, with no trace of the virus in her blood.

"I myself was healed of chronic headaches, which had developed from a head injury. Every day I took a large chunk of bread and chewed it bite-by-bite, meditating on the mystery of exchanging my sickness with Jesus' wholeness, because all my diseases were placed on Him. He paid the price for my wholeness."

THE SIN-BEARING MESSIAH ALSO TOOK OUR SICKNESSES

John also researched Isaiah's prophecy about the sin-bearing Messiah. "The ancient rabbis believed that Isaiah 53, written 700 years before the birth of Jesus, described a coming Messiah who would take our sins and our sicknesses onto His own body. They called this Messiah the Leprous Messiah because He would be disfigured by the sins of humanity. They saw in the passage that He would be a source of healing as well as forgiveness of sin."

> *"But He was pierced through for our transgres-*
> *sions, He was crushed for our iniquities;*
> *The chastening for our well-being fell upon Him,*
> *and by His stripes we are healed"* (Isaiah 53:5).

John continues: "Note that the prophecy says, '...by His stripes, we are healed' (Isa. 53:5). Part of this passage is repeated in Matthew 8:17 and again in First Peter 2:24 because it is so important. The stripes referred to were 39 lashes that were laid on His back when he was scourged prior to being crucified.

"Jesus' body was beaten in punishment for the sins of humanity. In becoming the Lamb of God, Jesus took the punishment for us, so we could be the righteousness of God in Him. It was not pointless suffering, but was something He accepted so that we could be healed, soul and body, according to prophecy. Isaiah 53:10 says that it pleased the Lord to bruise Him, and that He was made to be sick with our sicknesses and sin with our sins.

"The movie by Mel Gibson, *The Passion of the Christ*, does

not really portray how much abuse Jesus actually took. The Bible says that the lashes flayed His back so completely that it looked like one big stripe. His beard was plucked out and His face was beaten. Isaiah 53 gives a very graphic description of the beating He took when He became sin for us. He was made unrecognizable by the beating."

Both sin and sicknesses are works

of the devil.

Since He was made to be sick with our sicknesses, we shouldn't bear our own sicknesses any more than we should continue to bear our own sin. When it comes to redemption, it is wrong to separate sin and sickness. God wants the whole man—body, soul, and spirit—to be reconciled with Him. Both sin and sicknesses are works of the devil. Sin is his work against our spirit, and sickness is often his attack against our body.

THINK OF THE LORD'S SUPPER AS A KIND OF MEDICINE

John encourages people to think of the Lord's Supper as if it were medicine: "If you went to a doctor and got some pills, you would take them as directed, maybe two or three times a day, and you would not expect to be completely healed the first time you took them. I encourage people to place as much faith in the Lord's Supper as they do in their doctor's medicine. If you are sick, take the Lord's Supper like any other medicine. Every time you take it, meditate on the Lord's body, expecting gradual healing to manifest. Communion is yours to take as often as you feel led to do so. Your body is the temple of the Holy Spirit, and you are the priest, and you can observe Communion wherever and whenever you decide.

"Jesus said, 'What things so ever you desire, believe you receive it and you will have it.' In Communion you can believe that you are being progressively healed, and this takes the pressure off to receive healing all at once.

If we take Communion on a regular basis, daily or even several times a day, we can take it believing in progressive healing. This is good for people who do not have the faith to receive immediate, total healing, and it builds their faith because they can see small, progressive improvements. The important thing is to take the Lord's Supper in faith, recognizing signs of improvement.

WHAT YOU CAN DO

1. John encourages everyone to develop observance of the Lord's Supper as a way of life. If you are very sick, take it several times a day, just as you would take any other medicine.

2. You can observe the Lord's Supper by yourself, in your own home or wherever you are. The earliest followers of Jesus did it every day, going from house to house according to the book of Acts. You do not need to be in church or have a pastor present. In God's eyes, you are a priest. You are the temple of the Holy Spirit, so it is your privilege and your obligation to observe the Lord's Supper.

3. You do not need any special bread or wine, because it is your faith that is the key, not the material objects you use. Faith is the key to unlocking all of the promises of God. Jesus said, "What things so ever you desire, believe you receive them and you shall have them" (see Mark 11:24 KJV).

When we take Communion in faith, then we enter not only into forgiveness of sin, but also healing for our body.

4. John says, "I like to take a large hunk of bread so that I can chew it and meditate for a long time on this mystery. I have made a string with 39 knots on it, and as I chew the bread, I touch the knots thinking of the 39 lashes that Jesus took for me. This helps me to discern the Lord's body, and the freedom I now have because I have reconciliation with God. I think of my healing as something that is already done, already accomplished. As I eat the bread, I receive healing in every cell, every organ, and every function of my body.

5. "After taking communion, it is a very good time to cast out spirits of infirmity. We must not underestimate the role of evil spirits, because 11 of 19 individual healings that Jesus did involved casting out a spirit of infirmity. I like to think of doing spiritual warfare with the blood of Jesus on my breath."

FINAL THOUGHTS

"I have been privileged to bring the message of healing through the Lord's Supper in many parts of the world, and have had the great blessing of seeing all types of illness healed when people learn the truth. The truth is that every disease and every sin you can ever know has already been taken by Jesus, so you do not have to suffer it. Put your faith into receiving what Jesus did at Calvary. Think about it when you take the Lord's Supper, and have abundant life. Your only question should be whether your healing will come gradually or as a sudden miracle."

CHAPTER SEVEN

ONE OF THE GREATEST HEALING MIRACLES OF THE 20TH CENTURY

DELORES PASSED FROM PENDING DEATH TO ABUNDANT LIFE IN A KATHRYN KUHLMAN CONFERENCE, EVEN THOUGH SHE HAD NEVER BELIEVED IN DIVINE HEALING. SHE EXPERIENCED ONE OF THE GREAT HEALING MIRACLES OF THE 20TH CENTURY, AND WENT ON TO DEDICATE HER LIFE TO A MINISTRY OF HEALING.

D elores Winder was dying. Although she was just 48 years old, a bone disease that had tortured her life was now in its final stages. Her esophagus was ruptured, a fractured bone was poking through her skin, organs were failing, and the doctors said they could do no more for her. Delores was granted permission to leave the hospital so that she could die at home.

A Rare and Painful Disease

Delores's symptoms had begun in childhood; she seemed to break bones very easily. When she was in her late twenties, several vertebrae collapsed and had to be fused. The spinal fusion failed and had to be repeated three more times. Her doctors finally realized that something was terribly wrong with her bones.

Delores was ultimately diagnosed with a rare disease in which her bones thinned out because they could not absorb calcium and other needed minerals from her bloodstream. This made them old and brittle and as easy to break as a twig. Her hip sockets were so fragile that she could barely walk, and she lived in fear of them failing completely. As the disease progressed, she had to live in a full body cast with a neck brace to avoid more breakage.

———···●●———————————————●●···———

She could not walk without assistance, hold her own child, or enjoy anything like a normal life.

———···●●———————————————●●···———

Delores also had to take a lot of medication, and it made her sick and unable to eat. Toward the end, she weighed only 73 pounds. She was almost completely disabled and required help for the most simple body functions. It is hard to imagine living for 15 years in such a condition. She could not walk without assistance, hold her own child, or enjoy anything like a normal life.

One of the worst aspects was the excruciating pain. Delores described her normal pain level as "15 on a 10-point scale." Even the heaviest pain medications could not alleviate her suffering, so the doctors performed a serious surgical procedure, called a percutaneous chordotomy, in which they went into the brain and burned out the nerves to the lower part of her body. The good news was that the pain level was greatly reduced because of the procedure. The bad news was that her lower body now could feel nothing and could not move on its own. This procedure was an extreme measure, usually reserved for the terminally ill.

DELORES DID NOT FEAR DEATH

Delores was not afraid to die. She had been a Christian since childhood, and she loved God and believed in God, and knew her Bible well. However, her church taught that healing had passed away with the apostles. She believed that everything that happened to her was God's will, and that her job as a Christian was to bear her suffering as best she could.

The idea of dying did not bother her, but she was deeply grieved about leaving her husband and 14-year-old son all alone. She did not tell her son she was dying, but he knew; and she could hear him crying at night in his room. She said, "I begged God to tell me what would happen to my boy—how he would get along and be cared for after I was gone. I just wanted to be able to tell him and my husband, Bill, that it would be okay for them. That worry was the main thing I thought about. I prayed about it almost constantly, as I waited for my end to come."

Delores was not afraid to die.

JESUS SET ME FREE

"One day I was lying in my bed and a lady I knew as an acquaintance came into my bedroom. She had come to pray for me. While she was there, she turned on the TV to a show with Kathryn Kuhlman, the miracle-healing lady. I was just revolted by what I saw. I did not believe in divine healing at all, and I felt at the time that these television ministries were making a mockery of faith. I asked her to turn it off, and to please leave me. Well, she did turn it off, but she asked me just to pray about Miss Kuhlman and to not close any doors.

"Later, after she left, I was pleading with God to tell me

how He was going to take care of my son Chris and my husband. As I prayed, I clearly heard the name 'Kathryn Kuhlman' just as if someone had said it out loud. So I thought that my answer about Bill and Chris would come through her."

I felt at the time that these television ministries were making a mockery of faith.

It was not too long afterward that Miss Kuhlman came to a nearby town to speak on the Holy Spirit at a Methodist conference. Delores had a feeling that she must go to this conference to get her answer about Bill and Chris.

Although she was so desperately ill, her friend Gail agreed to take her to the conference. At first, it seemed like a wasted journey because she was so helpless that Gail was unable to get her out of the car. They had decided to give up and go back home when a man came out of the meeting and offered to help. He lifted her out of the car, carried her into the service, and got her and Gail settled in their seats.

Delores had her answer...

KATHRYN INTRODUCES THE HOLY SPIRIT

Kathryn Kuhlman came to the stage and began to teach saying, "I am going to introduce you to the Holy Spirit. If you call the Holy Spirit *it*, you don't know Him. He is, *God here with us*. He is the third Person of the trinity." That is the last thing Delores heard, because she suddenly felt that she was in the presence of God. A great sense of peace washed over her, and she had a vision. In the vision, she saw her son standing with a man that she recognized as Jesus. Jesus told her that her son need never feel alone, that He would always be with him.

Delores had her answer; she had what she had come to the conference to receive.

Delores later said, "I had been in church all my life, and had even taught Sunday School. I read my Bible constantly, but the reality of the Holy Spirit had always escaped me. He is so real, and He wants us to know Him as a person—to be conscious of Him in everything we do. He wants to use all of us to deliver gifts of healing. All we have to do is open our hearts to Him. Healing is the ministry of the Church, and He wants to use all of us for this purpose."

All these insights were to come later on. At the time of Kathryn's service, Delores only knew that she had met the Holy Spirit, and she had the peace she had been seeking about her family. Meanwhile, people in the audience were being touched. Some seemed to faint, some were getting healed, and others were laughing. Although Delores had encountered the Holy Spirit in a very personal way, she wanted no part of a healing service, which she thought was a lot of bunk. She was ready to leave and was pulling herself to the edge of the seat, gathering her things. Suddenly, her legs started burning as if they were on fire. This made her even more desperate to leave. Delores did not realize that her legs were supposed to be dead, and medically speaking, they had no potential to feel burning pain. Something supernatural was happening to Delores, and she did not even recognize it!

Surprised by Healing

Delores described what happened next: "I wanted no part of the healing sideshow. My friend was helping me get up to leave, when I noticed a man standing next to me. He said, 'Something is happening to you.' I told him, 'My legs are burning like fire, and I am dying, and I need to get out of here right now.'"

"My legs are burning like fire, and I am dying, and I need to get out of here right now."

He helped her up, and as he helped her shuffle to the door, he asked her if she had had any surgeries. She told him a short version of her medical condition, including the pain-deadening surgery. The man then asked how she could feel her legs burning if she had had her nerves deadened!

Delores then heard the man say that he had come off the stage to her because he knew she was being healed. At first she thought this was just too hard to believe, but there was something in his face that said, *He knows what he is talking about.* Despite her misgivings, he persuaded her to take off her body cast, and allow herself to be carried to the stage to meet personally with Kathryn Kuhlman. There, her greatest joy and worst fear came to pass. She found herself being held up to stand with Kathryn in front of 3,000 people, the center of a big spectacle.

"I was completely healed!"

Kathryn told her to walk, and the men holding her up backed away. Terrified of falling, she tried to prove she could not move her feet. To her amazement, her feet did move, and she started walking. Suddenly, she could feel the floor! Then the feeling came back into her hands and arms, and she started shouting, "I can feel! I can feel!" Later they told her she began running around the stage. When she came back, Kathryn told her to bend over, and she did so, finding her spine was completely healed. She could touch the floor with no pain and was able to stand up. Everything was different! Different! Kathryn smiled at her and said, "There is work for you to do. God wants you to have a dose of the Holy Spirit." Kathryn laid hands on her, and she went down from the power of the Holy Spirit.

Delores said, "When we left, I walked off that platform—no cast, no cane, no assistance. This was medically impossible. I had thought the woman was a kook, but I was healed. I was in such shock that I did not really know what had happened. But I was completely healed!"

When Delores finally arrived home, it was 2 A.M. Her son had been waiting up for her and came to the door. He saw his mother get out of a car unassisted for the first time in his life. He was so excited he ran to her and picked her up, all 73 pounds of her, and began dancing around with her. Her husband was in shock, but really thought somehow it would not last. He made up his mind to enjoy it as long as it lasted. The next morning Delores got up and took a shower by herself for the first time in many, many years. She went to church and then went out to lunch, where she ate a normal meal for the first time in years. She went back to the same doctor who had sent her home to die. When he confirmed that she was completely well, she said, "Is there any possible medical explanation for this?" And there wasn't. It was God.

Growing Into a Miracle

It took Delores a long time to process what happened to her. She had never believed in healing at all and was disturbed because she could not explain what had happened. Gradually, she began to understand, however. As she got to know the Holy Spirit, she started to have quite a number of supernatural experiences, signs, and healing miracles coming through her.

Delores said, "God has given a healing ministry to the whole Church, not just to special people. It is the work of the Holy Spirit, but we must step out and take a chance to pray for people. I often wonder what would have happened if that man had not stepped forward to help me out of the car. We should all be doing these works. If people will only open their hearts, God will do it. We just have to believe. And if we cannot believe, we can pray, 'Lord, I do believe in You, help my unbelief.' My belief was always in Jesus, not in healing."

Delores Rebels Against Healing

Although she was overjoyed at being healed, Delores struggled because she could not explain it. People who knew how sick she had been were shocked at her vibrant recovery and wanted to know how it happened, and why it had happened. She said, "People that knew how sick I had been did not know what to think about my healing and wanted answers. I had no answers, and did not know what to think of it myself. I really had believed that divine healing ended with Jesus and the apostles. Also, I didn't want to be any kind of spectacle at all. I wanted no part of the divine healing movement because of the way I had seen it portrayed on television."

Delores tried to stay home and mind her own business doing housework and taking care of her family for the first time in more than a decade. But her phone kept ringing with people calling to talk about her miracle. She got to the point of not answering her phone and even asked her husband if they could move away someplace so that she could go back to being anonymous. She really wanted no part of the divine healing movement.

Her husband counseled her to stay where she was and see what the Lord would have her do. Her healing had come for a reason.

People began to show up at her house seeking prayer for their own healing. She always tried to help them as best she could because she understood the desperation that the very sick sometimes feel. Also, strange things were happening when she tried to help people. She was hearing words and getting images about people's conditions that really confused her, but when she prayed in accordance with these images, people were healed.

Her healing had come for a reason.

For example, a lady came to her house asking for prayer, seeming desperate but not really indicating the nature of her problem. Delores suddenly saw an image of this woman in a lesbian relationship. She was so shocked by this image that she wondered if it were from the devil. Then suddenly it was written on the palm of her hand what she had to say to the woman. To her amazement, the woman received her message and came back later and told her about the tremendous work God had done in her life.

After the lady left, Delores started to write down what

she had seen written on her palm so that she could use it when others came, but the Lord spoke to her and said that she must trust Him to lead her in each situation and not try to pre-plan it.

Other strange things were happening also. Delores said, "I would get hot spots on my hands, and when it happened I would put my hands in my pockets and hide them. One day I was at Bible study when I got these hot spots. We were all standing up after class, and as I reached out to help another lady get up from her chair, she took hold of my hand. As soon as she touched my hand, she fell down onto another person. I reached out to help this other lady get up, and she also fell over. Then I backed up and accidentally touched two others who also fell down in the Spirit. I was so upset about this that I rushed to leave and I brushed against a lady who was in a wheelchair, and I was later told she came out of that wheelchair."

THE GIFTS OF THE HOLY SPIRIT ARE FOR TODAY

Although Delores had been a Christian all her life, she had never had any teaching about the power gifts of the Holy Spirit. In fact, she had been taught that they did not exist and firmly believed it.

A friend led her to visit a pastor who could help her understand the workings of the Holy Spirit. At first she argued with the pastor, saying, "These gifts are not for today—they passed away with the apostles." The pastor challenged her to show him where in the Bible it said that the gifts were not for today, and she couldn't find a single place where it said the age of miracles had passed. Her eyes were opened to great teaching passages that said, "Greater works than these shall you do" (see John 14:12). And, "Nothing shall be impossible to you" (see Matt. 17:20; Luke 1:37). She saw how Paul, not one of the original apostles, did great miracles, and how the early churches that he founded were based on supernatural manifestations of the Holy Spirit. One thing about Delores, she respected the Word of God. A light went on inside, and she heard the voice of the Lord saying to her, "I have taken your theology away."

Delores said, "We have a watered-down version of the Gospel. I am a prime example that God is the same Healer today that He was in Jesus' time. If people will only open their hearts to it, God will do the miracles. People have become so programmed to the worldly way that they will not believe the truth of the Gospel. This is exactly what happened to me. My prayer is that you begin to believe, and ask the Lord to help your unbelief."

———··•• ◀—————————▶ ••··———

Although Delores had been a

Christian all her life, she had never

had any teaching about the power

gifts of the Holy Spirit.

———··•• ◀—————————▶ ••··———

BELIEF MATTERS

What you believe is important. If you seek healing, you must believe that God exists and that healing is for today as much as when Jesus walked the earth. Delores teaches, "Beware of the natural mind. It is programmed with all sorts of unbelief, and belief in the wrong things. The natural man is programmed to believe that cancer is a fatal disease and very often even the treatment kills. But cancer can be healed. It does not always turn out the way the doctors say it will. In my Bible study, we believe what the

Scriptures teach, not what humankind teaches, and we get results when we pray.

"For example, a doctor's wife came to our Bible study with cancer throughout her body. Being a doctor's wife, she had plenty of medical tests that documented the seriousness of her condition. The people in our Bible study were prepared to pray for her, so we prayed and anointed her with oil. Her healing was not immediately apparent, but three months after we prayed for her, she had a CAT scan that showed the cancer had gone completely away."

We get results when we pray.

Delores does not say to disregard medical advice. She believes that medical care is important. Delores teaches that what we should get rid of is our unbelief.

"The mind of Messiah Jesus says our body is the temple of

the Holy Spirit (see 1 Cor. 6:19). He needs to dwell in it. When He does, cancer gets pushed out. Our purpose should be to walk in the presence of the Holy Spirit, and to care for our bodies as the temple of the Holy Spirit.

"We get so programmed with the world's way of thinking that we cannot easily believe in healing. What does work is to get so saturated with Jesus and so far away from the world you know that you know you are healed.

"God uses doctors, and He uses surgery. We must be open to medical help, but we should go to God first."

YOU CAN BE A HEALER

"Jesus is the same yesterday, today, and tomorrow. When He walked the earth, He healed the sick, cast out demons, and raised the dead. This was His ministry. He passed it on to His disciples, telling them to go make disciples of all nations and to pass this ministry on (see Matt. 28:19). He came to bring us abundant life. We miss this abundance because we are not expecting it. We have lived in the natural realm so long that we have forgotten that we also live in the spiritual realm. God can use anyone who is willing to be used to pass on these gifts of healing. If you are filled with the Holy Spirit, you lay hands on the sick and you expect that the Holy Spirit will heal them.

"Healing gifts belong to the Holy Spirit, not the person. So if someone is sick, you should not wait for a healer to come on the scene, but you should lay hands on the sick yourself and expect—expect—that they will be healed."

God can use anyone who is willing to

be used to pass on these gifts of healing.

To illustrate this, Delores described an experience she had while ministering at a Presbyterian church in Shreveport, Louisiana. Although the audience was filled with people seeking healing, Delores found her attention particularly drawn to a Catholic Sister sitting in the audience. She felt impressed to invite the Sister onto the stage to minister with her, and the Sister agreed. Delores asked her to pray for a woman with a large, disfiguring growth on her face. The Sister looked startled, and said, "I've never done this before, but I will try."

"No," Delores told her. "You will not try, you will do! Then God does the rest." The Sister laid her hand on the woman's cheek and prayed. When she took her hand away, the disfiguring growth was gone. The first time this Catholic Sister prayed for someone, a great miracle was done through her!

———··•◆————————————◆•··———

The first time this Catholic Sister

prayed for someone, a great miracle

was done through her!

———··•◆————————————◆•··———

"Always know it is the Holy Spirit doing the work. We are just the messengers. This is the beginning of a great day in the church, where the Lord is pouring out His Spirit on all flesh. More and more churches will be carrying out the full ministry of Jesus, and healing ministries like mine will no longer be needed. The healing ministry will have returned to the Church where it belongs.

"Right now I know that God is changing hearts, preparing those hearts to believe in healing and be willing to be used. This is the cry of my heart, to see changed lives. This is the work of the Church, to set people free.

"I prayed for a man in one of my services who couldn't walk. To make a long story short, I took away his cane and he started walking, then running around the sanctuary. This man is now a minister in India, serving God."

Often we have to make an effort to step out in some way. God will honor it.

SPIRITUAL WEAPONS

One thing that comes through Delores's teaching is that the spirit is the primary battleground on which we must fight. Our security is trusting in the Word of God. She says that we must literally put on a new mind, seeing our bodies as the temple of the Holy Spirit. Welcoming His presence pushes disease out of us. With our hearts firmly anchored in the truth of God's Word, we can better see how to fight off diseases that may attack us. This understanding helped Delores fight off a return of her deadly symptoms.

Although Delores had been healed at the Kathryn

Kuhlman service, in the back of her mind was a fear that her disease would return, bringing back misery and suffering. About a year after her healing, Delores was home doing housework when she was struck with a sharp pain in her back. The pain struck in the same place where she had had a spinal fusion years ago. Her first thought was that her healing was lost and that she would go back to her terminally ill state; she had heard stories of people who had lost their healing. As she prayed for guidance, she realized that this was an attack—the devil was trying to steal her healing. When she realized the nature of the attack, she began singing and praising the Lord, rebuking the symptoms in the name of Jesus. The pain went completely away, and did not return.

Another powerful principle that she teaches is to believe that once you have asked, that you have received, even if it is not immediately manifested. Delores teaches that healing is a process that sometimes comes about gradually. We must be patient as it comes into manifestation. In her book, *Surprised by Healing*, Delores says, "When we know what God has available for us, then we can come to Him and ask for it. But we don't keep on asking. We start appropriating it. We say, 'Lord, although I still have pain in my body, I believe that You are healing me because Your Word says so. I believe I am healed according to your Word.' Then our physical body begins to change and the mind, body, and spirit come into accord with

God's Word. We must be in accord with His Word to be healed, for it is basically through His Word that we hear from Him.

"Most healing is not instant, but is a process that unfolds over time. Just keep saying, 'Thank you. Thank you, Lord. I am being healed.' Know that healing power is at work within you. God says all things are possible to those who believe. Believe it, and it will be."

THE CENTRALITY OF THE HOLY SPIRIT

"The Holy Spirit is my life. Jesus sent Him to be with us always, to lead us, guide us, and use us. Without Him, we are trying to live our lives by ourselves, without hope. We keep Him in the guest room of our heart. We must bring Him out of the guest room into the living room. We are not to do anything with Him, but we are to let Him do with us as He decides. Anything can happen. But we have to surrender totally to the Lordship of Jesus.

"In practical terms, it means I can't live without Him. In the beginning the Lord would say to me, 'Remember, you can't lift a finger without Me.' Today, I say, 'Jesus, You are my whole life. You lead me and guide me and direct me. Take me where You want me to go. Use me.' This does not mean He takes you out of your life. You are still in the same place, but He is fore-most in your mind and your thinking and your awareness. I am still primarily a housewife. I am a wife and a mother. I will never go into a downtown office building to minister. So it is very important for you to catch the vision to minister, to have the gifts in operation wherever you are, whatever you are doing in your daily life."[1]

ENDNOTE

1. Wherever she goes, Delores walks in signs and healing miracles. More details about her healing, her miracle experiences, and her teaching are revealed in her book, *Surprised by Healing* (Shippensburg, PA: Destiny Image, 2009).

God Always Has a Plan

Dale and Pearl Raatz beat a medically hopeless situation through skillfully applying the Word of God, but Dale had to hear God's plan before it all worked out. He calls God his "Commander in Chief." Here is their story.

PEARL FELL INTO A DEEP COMA

On a cold February evening in 1997, Dale and Pearl Raatz went to a church music program in Iron Mountain, Michigan. As they were taking off their coats in the warm church auditorium, Pearl fell over, crying, "My head! My head feels like it's exploding!" After crying out, she experienced convulsions, and then fell into a deep coma.

Dale describes what happened next: "While we waited for an ambulance, the other pastors and I laid hands on Pearl and prayed. My natural mind was numb from the shock of what was happening, but from deep within, I heard the words of Psalm 118:17, 'You shall live and not die, and declare the works of the Lord.'"

A RIVER OF LIVING WATER FLOWED OUT OF MY HEART

"I began to speak these words over my unconscious wife. I said them repeatedly, and by the time the ambulance came, I had an inner sense that I would see them come true. Pearl would live and not die, by the authority of the Word of God. This inner conviction became like a rock of truth that sustained me through many battles of faith until Pearl was completely healed.

"A friend went to the hospital with me, and while the doctors worked over Pearl, we waited in a nearby room. I was in the worst storm of my life, and I did the only thing that I knew to do. I lifted my hands and began worshiping God, thanking Him for His Word.

"As I worshiped, comfort came to me. My sense of shock and numbness gave way, and the rich deposit of God's Word came flowing out of my heart like a river of living water."

I Spoke God's Promises, Inserting Pearl's Name

"I began confessing some of the many promises for healing that the Scripture teaches, inserting Pearl's name in each one:

"'Jesus, Himself, bore our sins in His own body on the tree, that we, being dead to sins, should live unto righteousness. By His stripes Pearl was healed' (see 1 Pet. 2:24).

"'That it might be fulfilled which was spoken by Isaiah the

prophet, saying: Jesus, Himself, took Pearl's infirmities and bore her sicknesses' (see Matt. 8:17).

"'I call those things that be not, as though they were' (see Rom. 4:17).

"'I have the faith of God, and I speak to this mountain of physical destruction, commanding it, Be thou removed and be thou cast into the sea (see Mark 11:23).

"'God has highly exalted Jesus and given Him a name above every name, that at the name of Jesus every knee must bow. Every disease, every infirmity, every problem has to submit itself to the name of Jesus. And every tongue will confess that Jesus Christ is Lord to the glory of God' (see Phil. 2:9-11)."

YOUR WIFE WILL NEVER REGAIN CONSCIOUSNESS

"All through that night of waiting, I confessed these and other Scriptures. When I grew tired, my friend took over the job of speaking God's Word over Pearl's situation. When the doctors came out, they said, 'Your wife has had a massive stroke, and most likely will be dead within hours. If she does live, she will never regain consciousness, and will be totally paralyzed from the neck down.'

"'No! She will not die!' The words rang in my heart. 'By the Word of God, she will live and make a full recovery.' I told that to myself over and over. I have learned that fear brings the devil into situations, and that even a little bit of fear is a faith killer. It is faith that gets God's attention and brings His power into our needs. I resolved to stay in a faith position and to not be moved by fear."

No! She will not die!

The next day, the doctors moved Pearl to a larger hospital in Green Bay with more facilities for stroke patients. However, the new doctors gave Dale the same hopeless medical evaluation. One of them told him, "Our tests show that Pearl has suffered a catastrophic stoke, and large parts of her brain are totally destroyed. She will probably never come out of her coma, and even if she does, she will never recognize or remember you. I am sorry to have to tell you this, but there is no hope."

ABRAHAM HOPED AGAINST HOPE— HE IS THE FATHER OF FAITH

Dale said, "Maybe from a human perspective there is no hope, but where there is God, there is hope! He is the God of Abraham 'who against hope believed in hope, that he might become the father of many nations.' (Rom. 4:18 KJV). So, just as Abraham considered not his own body, now dead, I resolved to not consider Pearl's nearly lifeless body, but to meditate instead on the promises of God, and to continually speak them over my wife.

I knew her spirit could hear and gain strength, even though she remained in a coma.

"Because the situation seemed so discouraging, the doctors

delayed doing surgery that would relieve pressure on Pearl's brain. I felt that they were expecting her to die no matter what they did, so it was a minor triumph when they finally agreed to operate. I had strongly wished they would operate sooner, but the Bible says that faith works by love (see Gal. 5:6). For this reason, I knew that I could not get into strife with any of the medical people. Even when I was at odds with the medical people, I always tried to deal with them in love and kindness, and this brought about many small miracles.

"For example, I felt that it was important that Pearl be bathed constantly in anointed music and the Scriptures; so I wanted to bring in a tape recorder to play them 24 hours a day. The nurses told me that this was absolutely against the rules. But because my loving approach had brought me so much favor with the medical staff, they eventually bent those rules and allowed me to bring in a tape recorder. Soft worship music and reading of the Word filled Pearl's room 24 hours a day. I knew her spirit could hear and gain strength, even though she remained in a coma."

I Had to Hear God's Plan of Attack

Dale knew that getting Pearl back from this seemingly hopeless state was going to be a long fight. He said, "Through the past years, we had seen enough miracles come about through speaking God's Word that I really trusted it. However, I needed more. I needed to hear God's plan for this situation. He is the Commander in Chief, and I needed to know how He wanted me to fight this battle."

Lord, what are You trying to tell me?

BY PRAYING AND MEDITATING ON THE WORD, I COULD HEAR HIM

"By praying and meditating on the Word every day, I had long ago learned to discern His voice. I was continually listening for His guidance. One day, as I was reading Second Corinthians 5:17, 'Therefore, if any man be in Christ, he is a new creature,' I heard the voice of the Lord asking me what those words meant to me.

"The question really made me think, 'Lord, what are You

trying to tell me?' I began to realize that this passage was not limited to the spiritual side of things, but that Pearl was also a new creature physically in Christ. Therefore, she could have a new brain!"

Dale began to call this new brain into being. He persistently spoke to Pearl, as she lay in her coma, saying, "You are a new creature in Christ and you have a new brain." The Lord also showed Dale that the name of Jesus was higher than any other name, and that every knee must bow to that name (see Phil. 2:9). He began to speak directly to the name "stroke" and demand that it bow to the name of Jesus. He describes the remarkable story of this battle in his book, *The God of Now.*

Dale Prayed for Others Who Were Healed

Dale stayed in the hospital with Pearl, night and day for

several weeks, continuously fighting on her behalf. During this time, he prayed for some other "hopeless" cases in the hospital and saw healing miracles that saved lives and brought the reality of God for those patients and their families.

PEARL HAS OPENED HER EYES!

He was in another patient's room, praying for that person's healing on the day when Pearl finally opened her eyes, recognized her family, and began to speak. He said, "When my children came to tell me Pearl had opened her eyes, I was overjoyed, but I was not surprised. The Word of God is a seed that will always bring forth a harvest if we follow the guidelines laid out in Mark 11:22-26."

> *And Jesus answering saith unto them, Have faith in God. For verily I say unto you, That whosoever shall say unto this mountain, Be thou removed, and be thou cast into the sea; and shall not doubt in his heart, but shall believe that those things which he saith shall come to pass; he shall have whatsoever he saith. Therefore, I say unto you, What things so ever ye desire, when ye pray, believe that ye receive them, and ye shall have them.*
>
> *And when ye stand praying, forgive, if ye*

have ought against any: that your Father also
which is in heaven may forgive you your tres-
passes.

PEARL IS COMPLETELY WELL

The Word worked for Pearl. Pearl mended quickly, and today she is completely well. She is vibrant and alive, and ministers healing to others along with Dale.

WHAT YOU CAN DO

Pearl is among us today because Dale knew how to apply the Word of God. Here is what he recommends people do in a crisis situation:

1. From the first moment, resolve to believe that God's Word is true, no matter what medical facts you face. Know that the Scriptures teach that God wants you well.

2. You do not have to refuse medical care. God has a plan, and it may involve doctors. For those who feel that they have to choose between trusting God's Word and accepting medical care, Dale advises, "If something is good and helpful, it is wrong to turn it away. God has given us medicine; we must use it in faith, always understanding that God is the One who heals."

3. Faith works through love, so make sure you stay in a loving attitude toward hospital personnel and others. Getting drawn into

aggravation and irritability is as unwise as getting into fear.

4. Speak the promises of God continuously, and let no doubt or unbelief come out of your mouth. Tell others about your beliefs. We can't explain why God places such an emphasis on the spoken word, but He does.

5. Praise and worship God in the midst of the storm. This will not only bring you comfort, but it will also stir up your faith and bring God onto the scene.

6. Pray and meditate on God's Word, listening for His battle plan. He already knows how He wants to work. Our job is to hear that plan.

CLOSING THOUGHTS

Dale said, "God raised my wife up from a brain-dead condition, and has proven to me that He will perform His Word for any of us, in any situation that we face in life. However, we must position ourselves to receive from Him. My heart is to let you know that this is not just for selected people. You can also learn how to bring God's power into your situation."

CHAPTER NINE

A DOCTOR EXPERIENCES DIVINE HEALING

DR. TOM RENFRO AND HIS WIFE SID WERE BLIND-SIDED WHEN HE WAS DIAGNOSED WITH TERMINAL CANCER. TODAY HE IS WELL, BACK TO PRACTICING MEDICINE, AND PRAYING FOR THE SICK, OFTEN WITH MIRACULOUS RESULTS. HE SHARES WHAT HE HAS LEARNED AND HOW HE WAS HEALED.

Dr. Tom Renfro was born in 1955 in the rugged, coal-mining region of Virginia. After he finished his training in internal medicine, he returned to his hometown of Norton to set up a medical practice and raise his family. For a long time, things were going pretty well. His wife, Sid, had set up her own small business and his son Jason was finishing high school.

My Worst Fear Comes to Pass

Tom was shaving one morning in October of 1996, when he noticed a marble-sized lump on the back of his neck. By the end of October, other glands had swollen under both of his arms. That is when he knew something was seriously wrong.

Tom said, "My worst fear was that it might be some kind of lymphoma—cancer of the lymph system. I had treated a number of people with lymphoma, and I knew it to be a cruel disease. I immediately went to see my family doctor. He was worried too, and he ordered a biopsy of the lumps.

"The results were not good. I had a rare, particularly aggressive cancer of the lymph system, called mantel cell lymphoma. One of the world's leading authorities on lymphoma, Dr. Charles Hess, was on the staff at the medical school at the University of Virginia in Charlottesville. I went to see him, only to find that there was no medical hope, not even with experimental treatments."

That is when he knew something

was seriously wrong.

JESUS HEALED EVERYONE WHO CAME TO HIM

Tom said, "I had been given a death sentence, but something just rose up in me. I knew that this whole thing was wrong. I believed that God was good and loving. I had prayed for my patients often, and seen Him save people. Since medicine had no answers for me, I determined that I would see what help I could find in God."

Tom began to meet with his pastors to study what the Bible actually said about healing. Tom said, "As we read the Gospels together, I saw that Jesus had healed everyone who came to Him. He healed people both in large crowds and individually.

Since medicine had no answers

for me, I determined that I

would see what help

I could find in God.

"I saw that healing power flowed out of Jesus to all who were able to press close enough to touch Him. He never turned anyone away who asked Him for healing. It seemed to me so obvious that God wanted to heal people of sickness that I started to wonder how I could have not seen it before."

The Devil Was Trying to Kill Me, Not God

"The lights really went on for me when I read John, chapter 10. There, Jesus says, 'The thief comes to steal, to kill and to destroy, but I am come that you might have life, and have it abundantly' (see John 10:10). I began to meditate on that. All day long I thought about those words: 'I am come that you might have life.'

"It wasn't God's will for me to die horribly. The devil was a thief. The devil was stealing my health and destroying the happiness of my family and friends. He was trying to kill me."

Facts Are Just Moments in Time— Truth Is Eternal

"I faced a dilemma about how to think about my situation. On the one hand, I had built my entire professional life on understanding natural law and medical science. On the other hand, the Bible plainly said it was not God's will for me to die, but to have life and have it abundantly. The Bible said, 'You shall know the truth, and the truth shall make you free' (John 8:32).

"I began to realize that there is a vast difference between facts and truth. Facts are just shadows, passing moments in time that take account of the past and present but not the future. Facts may change. Truth, on the other hand, is eternal and unchanging. Facts set limits, but the truth makes you free. I began to wonder how to lay hold of that truth so that I could be free."

Facts may change. Truth, on the other hand, is eternal and unchanging.

MY REAL BATTLE WAS AGAINST THE SPIRITUAL FORCES OF UNBELIEF

"I studied the great teaching in the sixth chapter of the Book of Ephesians which says, 'We do not battle against flesh and blood, but against powers and spiritual forces' (see Eph. 6:12). As I meditated on these and other Scriptures, I realized that my real battle was not against cancer, but against the spiritual forces who wanted to steal everything from me, then kill and destroy me, and wipe out my family in the process. All the powers of hell would line up to keep me from effectively believing the Word of God."

Tom said, "I knew that if the devil was fighting me, I would have to fight back. The devil was throwing pain and all kinds of symptoms at me to keep me from believing the promise of God. I fought back by meditating on God's promises, night and day, not only concentrating on specific Bible verses but also taking time to worship and praise and thank Him for all His goodness. The worship time grew to be extremely important to me. In addition, I read books about healing and listened to tapes about people who had been healed. I taught classes at my church on healing, and prayed for anyone who would let me do it.

I fought back by meditating on

God's promises, night and day . . .

"The Lord showed me one time that it was a little like a blacktop road with a yellow line down the middle. One side was the natural side with medical facts, my fears, and my concerns. On the other side was the Lord, where there was peace because He was taking care of things. The Lord showed me clearly that I must pick which side to walk on, and not try to walk on both. In the beginning, I often found myself weaving back and forth across the yellow line. When I would veer to the natural side, my understanding side, the medical side, I would catch myself, and pull my thinking back on the Lord's side. As time progressed, I walked more and more on the Lord's side."

PHYSICAL AND EMOTIONAL EXHAUSTION

"My struggle to find healing lasted for a long time. I became terribly sick and almost died on several occasions. My wife kept me alive, and she paid a hard price in both physical and emotional exhaustion. Our church was a lifeline. Their kindness, prayers, and support enabled us both to keep going."

The power of the church to sustain Tom was so great that he would drag himself to service no matter how sick he was. He realized one of his purposes on earth was to worship the

Lord, and even in a state of sickness, he was still going to release his worship unto God. Sickness wanted to suppress his worship, but praise in the midst of tribulation touches God. Sid and his family did whatever physically they had to do to get him to church to worship the Lord.

He realized one of his purposes on earth was to worship the Lord...

I Released My Spirit to the Lord

Tom said, "I was convinced that God's Word would not fail, even though the disease was ravaging my body. During the Thanksgiving holiday of 1997, my strength was nearly gone. My lungs were tightening up, and drawing each breath was a struggle. One night I was so exhausted that I couldn't fight anymore to keep breathing. My wife was exhausted and had fallen asleep beside me.

"I wasn't going to awaken her again. I prayed, thanking God for everything He was, and for everything He had done for me. I confessed to Him that I was physically exhausted and didn't have any more strength. I was going to sleep, I told Him, and that I would wake up in Heaven or in my bed, but for Him to be with me was what mattered. I released my spirit into the hands of God that night. I expected to die, but instead of dying, I had the most wonderful, refreshing, reviving rest."

I Knew That Healing Had Touched Me

"Shortly after that experience, I was meditating on the Lord and praying. I felt the healing touch of God come into my body. Nothing had physically changed, but I knew that I knew that healing had touched me. I was healed at that moment, but nothing physically seemed different."

I Learned to Depend Entirely on the Lord and Do What He Said

Tom said, "My attitude changed as well. I stopped fighting for myself. I learned to depend entirely on the Lord, to listen to Him and do what He said. The Lord gave me some very specific instructions. He told me first to put my financial affairs in order and to make out a will. After that, I was supposed to present myself for chemotherapy.

"Neither one of these things made sense to me, because if I were healed, then I wouldn't need either a will or chemotherapy. However, I determined to trust the Lord and not to depend on my own understanding, and I did as I had been directed."

LIFE EXPLODED INSIDE ME!

On December 1, 1997, Tom was taken by ambulance to Holston Valley Medical Center, in Kingsport, Tennessee. His breathing was very labored. Everyone assumed that he was very near to death, and that treatment was pointless. The medical staff said that the chemotherapy could possibly kill him immediately due to his weakened condition. Tom said, "We believed, however, that God had sent us here and would have the right person with the right treatment for us. At our insistence, they started the drug infusion."

Tom said, "When they hooked up the IV line for the chemotherapy, something amazing happened. In the instant that the drug hit my blood stream, I felt life exploding inside me. Chemotherapy uses poisons to attack tumors and usually it makes people very sick. However, I didn't feel that. I felt the life of God flooding through my body!

I felt the life of God flooding

through my body!

"Then I noticed something equally amazing happening with the tumors. Those hard, grapefruit-like balls that had covered my body and made my life so miserable had turned soft and mushy. Then they liquefied and melted away. They disappeared! It made me think of that Bible verse in the Psalms, which says, 'The hills melted like wax at the presence of the Lord' (see Ps. 97:5). That is just what happened.

"It is very unusual for chemotherapy to have such an immediate effect. Within hours those tumors were disappearing before our eyes."

I Became Contagious With God

The touch Tom had from the Lord was apparent to

everyone. Tom said, "God had touched me, and He made me infectious with Life! I became infectious with God, and I couldn't stop myself from sharing this joy. Though I was too weak to walk or dress myself, I went into the lobby of the oncology ward and told everyone passing through what had happened to me. I had to tell them about the great goodness of God. I believe at that time, I had supernatural strength, life, and joy. The Scripture had not failed: You will not die, but live and declare the works of the Lord" (see Ps. 118:17).

Tom's dramatic healing was a great witness of God's mighty power to the medical staff. Tom said, "Of the three doctors taking care of me, two had expected the chemotherapy to kill me. The third was more optimistic, and he thought it would take three rounds of chemo to cause even a 50 percent shrinkage of the tumors. Even when chemotherapy works, it works slowly. None of them expected what happened. It really messed them up."

MANY YEARS LATER

It has been many years since Tom was healed. Sid has an active ministry of outreach to caregivers, and Tom is back at work practicing medicine. He has a new understanding of what patients go through and also of what the Lord can do.

He and his wife have a full schedule traveling to teach the truth of the Lord's present-day willingness to heal.

I can never predict what God is going

to do in any given situation, but

I have prayed for people

given up to die, who were on

life support, and have seen them

come off life support and

walk out of the hospital.

Wherever they go, Tom and Sid pray for the sick. Tom said, "I can never predict what God is going to do in any given situation, but I have prayed for people given up to die, who were on life support, and have seen them come off life support and walk out of the hospital. I have prayed for people on chronic dialysis, and some have regained their renal function and ended dialysis. I have prayed for people with metastatic cancer and have seen that disease disappear. We serve an awesome God, and there is nothing He can't do."

Tom looks back on his battle as a spiritual journey. He believes he started out trying to believe in God's ability to heal, but really trusting in his own strength. He did everything he could to bring healing into his body, but it didn't manifest until he was touched by the Holy Spirit. "Then," he said, "I stopped trying to put in place my own formula for how God would heal me. I stopped claiming the gift, and I met up with the Giver."

IT DOES NOT HAVE TO BE INVISIBLE TO BE GOD WORKING

Many people have asked Tom why he waited so long to take chemotherapy, and how he can be sure it was God who healed him and not just the medicine. Tom answers, "We don't want to make the mistake of telling God how to be God. I would have preferred to be healed the first week, or anywhere along the way, but God heals people in His own way. The battle was God's, not mine.

"I didn't go for chemotherapy in the beginning because I didn't have a release in my spirit to do so. The risks of chemotherapy in my case outweighed the benefits of taking it. I firmly believe that if I had taken it early on, before God said to, it would have killed me. Also, the 300 medical staff who witnessed the miracle of my healing would have been denied that opportunity.

Also, the 300 medical staff who witnessed the miracle of my healing would have been denied that opportunity.

"God is the Healer, period. Healing is one of those things that remains within the divine province or authority of God. Sometimes God uses medicine and doctors to heal. It doesn't have to be 100 percent invisible to be God working. There was no one formula or method that Jesus used for healing people. And in the Old Testament, God directed Isaiah to put a poultice on Hezekiah to cure him.

"The important thing is to seek the Lord, to learn to listen to God, to believe Him and trust in Him, and to do what He tells you. Being a warrior for God does not mean fighting one great big battle. It starts right now, with making the next small decision about what to do. It is all about letting God be in charge."

A MESSAGE FROM TOM'S PASTORS

Tom's pastors, Glen Sturgill and Robert Fultz Jr., are men with many years of experience pastoring a faith-based church, and were a faithful, constant presence in the Renfros' lives. Pastor Sturgill said, "I have seen God move for many people who were dying. It is when people completely surrender and touch Him that they can really believe. It is like the woman with the hemorrhage in Mark 5 who said, 'If I can only touch the clothes of Jesus, then I will be healed' (see Mark 6:56). She touched Him, and she got what she needed. It isn't hard. Don't make it something difficult. Just believe in Him and seek Him until you touch Him. If you press in so close to Jesus that you bump into Him, His healing virtue will just jump onto you. I guarantee it." (See Resources in the back of the book for Renfro's contact information.)

CHAPTER TEN

DO SOMETHING EXTRA!

WHEN THE OBSTETRICIAN TOLD DR. GARY HILL AND HIS WIFE MARIE THAT THEIR UNBORN CHILD WOULD BE SEVERELY BRAIN DAMAGED, THEY REFUSED TO ACCEPT IT. THEY BELIEVED GOD WOULD HEAL THEIR UNBORN BABY, BUT THEY KNEW THEY WOULD HAVE TO FIND THE FAITH TO DO SOMETHING OUT OF THE ORDINARY TO GET A MIRACLE. HERE'S WHAT THEY DID.

More Than Half of Our Baby's Brain Was Missing

In the late fall of 1992, Dr. Gary Hill was an emergency medicine physician in Edmonton, Alberta, in western Canada. His wife, Marie, was within a few weeks of delivering their fourth child. They were happy, expectant parents. That is, until they were suddenly plunged into a life or death battle for the survival of their unborn baby. Marie describes how the storm blew up:

"I was expecting my fourth child. That day, I had gone to have an ultrasound, because at eight months, the baby still was not moving around, and seemed unusually small. I did not really suspect that anything serious was wrong with the baby. However, I began to be concerned when I saw that the doctor looked worried and wanted to do a second ultrasound. At the end of the second ultrasound, the doctor took a deep breath and started struggling for words. Finally he said, 'Well, your baby has eyes, a nose, and a mouth....'

"I saw that the doctor had a very grave and sad expression

on his face. He was saying that the baby had eyes and a mouth. What didn't my baby have? I suddenly felt terrified. I could not take any more anxiety and knew that I had to get out of there and get home. Although I was probably too upset to be driving, I raced home to talk to Gary. I told Gary to call the obstetrician right away because something terrible seemed to be wrong with the baby."

"Call the obstetrician right away—

something terrible seems to be

wrong with the baby!"

Gary wasted no time getting in touch with the doctor. He said, "Although I knew something was wrong, my worst fears did not prepare me for the shock I received when I got to his office and the doctor silently handed me my baby's ultrasound image. By looking at the ultrasound image, I could see immediately that more than half of my baby's brain was missing."

ABORTION WAS NOT AN OPTION

"The doctor explained it to me as kindly as he could, saying, 'I'm so sorry, Gary. Your baby has had an intrauterine stroke. The entire left hemisphere of her brain is gone. All that is left is a large cyst filled with fluid and some stray bits of tissue. She will probably die at birth. If she lives, she will be severely retarded and paralyzed on one side of her body. She will be unable to talk and will have a seizure disorder. One side of her body will not grow normally.' He was pronouncing a death sentence on my unborn child!"

Your baby has had an intrauterine stroke. The entire left hemisphere of her brain is gone.

Gary continues: "I was shocked and stunned. I asked a few more medical questions, but inwardly I was reeling. I could see the results of the ultrasound for myself, but I couldn't believe what I was seeing, or even comprehend what the doctor was saying at first.

"I just sat there in his office, staring at the ultrasound, trying to make sense of what was happening. Then the obstetrician raised the issue of terminating the pregnancy! I knew he was trying to be kind in making this offer, but it made me really angry. I stared at him for a moment and then said, 'Doctor, I am a Christian. I do not believe in abortion.'"

God Will Get Me Out of This... Somehow

"Although I did not believe in abortion, I was a medical doctor. I knew that the personal consequences of bringing such a damaged child into the world would be intense. I also knew that there was absolutely no medical answer for my baby's problem. There was no power on earth that could give my daughter a new brain.

"As I sat there in silence with the obstetrician, not sure of what to say next, something rose up inside of me. I looked straight at him. Then I said, 'There has to be an answer. My God has never let me down. He will get me out of this somehow.' With that, I stood up and left the office and started the drive home."

There Is a God, and You Are Supposed to Seek Him!

"I dreaded facing Marie with this horrible information. When I finally saw her, I said, 'Marie, I realize you don't want to know the details, but it's bad. Really bad.' I went upstairs to my room to be alone and try to compose myself. As soon as I closed the door I fell to my knees and cried out to God, in the deepest pain I had ever experienced.

"At that moment I felt totally devastated and over-whelmed. As I collected myself, however, it became really, really clear to me that I needed a miracle, and the only hope we had for one of those was in God. I said to myself, 'Listen, buster, you have to get hold of yourself. There is a God, and you are supposed to seek Him. He will help you. Your daughter's life depends on it. You are going to do this.'

"I spoke out loud to God and said, 'The Scriptures teach that you are a strong tower and a fortress, an ever-present help in time of need. O God, fulfill your promise. This is my time of need.'"

As I collected myself, however, it became really, really clear to me that I needed a miracle, and the only hope we had for one of those was in God.

I KNEW I WOULD HAVE TO DO SOMETHING EXTRA

"I knew this was such a serious situation that halfway measures wouldn't work. I got my faith originally from the Bible, from reading about God and what He does. I knew that the people who had been healed by Jesus often did more than the ordinary. They did something extra.

"For example, there were people who pulled the tiles off the roof of a house so they could lower a paralyzed guy down to Jesus to be healed. The power of God was there that day to heal everyone, but this guy was the only one who was recorded as being healed. He did something extra; his faith is what got him healed.

I knew that I had to spend

100 percent of my time seeking

God if I were going to

save her life.

"Faith like that was needed to save my daughter. If I had to rip the roof off of a house to get to the Lord for healing, I would do it. I knew that I had to spend 100 percent of my time seeking God if I were going to save her life. There was so much at stake that I decided to leave my job as an emergency department physician and spend all of my waking hours on this battle."

WE LEARNED THAT FACTS AND TRUTH ARE TWO DIFFERENT THINGS

"Marie and I began an intense search for God's plan to save our daughter's life. We read the Bible day and night. We read books and listened to audiotapes about healing, trying to learn whatever we could. One teacher in particular talked about speaking Bible verses into bad situations. He taught the importance of recognizing the difference between the negative facts that might confront us and the eternal truth of God's promises. He taught that outcomes were influenced by what the person chose to believe and talk about. In fact, he was teaching the words spoken by the Messiah:

> "'For verily I say unto you, That whosoever shall say unto this mountain, Be thou removed, and be thou cast into the sea; and shall not doubt in his heart, but shall believe that those things which he saith shall come to pass; he shall have whatsoever he saith. Therefore I say unto you, What things soever ye desire, when ye pray, believe that ye receive them, and ye shall have them' (Mark 11:24 KJV).

"We pulled ourselves together and determined to stand on God's Word and not be afraid. We determined that if we had to stand for 6 trillion years and tell the devil that our baby was healed, then that's what we would do."

WE SPOKE GOD'S PROMISES 400 TIMES A DAY

Gary and Marie went through the Bible and wrote down every verse they could find that promised healthy children. They made a list of all these verses and read them all, six times a day. Each morning, noon, and evening, they would read each Scripture verse one time as it was written, and then say out loud what the personal meaning of that verse was.

Gary later said that the impact of spending so much time thinking about the Word of God was life-changing for him. One Scripture in particular referred to a prophecy about the Messiah from the book of Isaiah. It said:

> *He was wounded for our transgressions, he was bruised for our iniquities; the chastisement for our peace was upon Him, and by His stripes we are healed* (1 Peter 2:24).

Gary said, "When Marie and I read that particular verse, it seemed to jump off the page and to come alive inside us. We knew it was for us to apply in our situation. We decided to speak that verse over our situation intensively. We quoted that verse and said, 'By His stripes, our baby is healed,' four hundred times a day." Gary remembers using his son's abacus, moving the beads of the ancient counting machine, one at a time, so he could make sure to keep his focus.

IS THE WORD OF GOD TRUE OR IS IT NOT?

Gary said, "It may not sound difficult to focus so intensively on God's Word, but it is. For one thing, you get tired. For another, part of you wants to give in and quit, and just accept whatever happens. A seductive voice seemed to call to me to quit trying. Over and over it said, 'Just give up. You can't do this. You don't know anybody who has ever done this. It won't work.' This voice played on my doubts and fears as if it were trying to weaken me.

"The worst moments were when I would wake up in the middle of the night and recall the image of my daughter's destroyed brain on the ultrasound. I would hear the words *severely retarded, paralyzed,* and *seizure disorder* pronounced by the obstetrician. I would imagine the difficult life my daughter would have if she were born so severely handicapped and wonder how my family would cope with such a situation. I would find my thoughts wandering to cases of Christians who had confessed healing Scriptures and then died anyway, and I worried about the lack of any progress.

I would find my thoughts

wandering to cases of

Christians who had confessed

healing Scriptures and

then died anyway . . .

"Being alone with thoughts such as these at 4:00 in the morning, I was forced to wrestle for my daughter's life with my own deepest fears and doubts. What I found at the bottom of all these thoughts was a basic question. Is the Word of God true or isn't it?"

WHAT ABOUT THE EXPERIENCES OF OTHERS?

"I realized I couldn't explain the experiences of other people. The only hope my daughter had was if I believed the Word of God just as it is written and to accept it for my situation. I just determined to believe the Bible over every other thing my mind could throw at me.

To feel the anxiety and fear lifting as I worshiped God was nothing short of awesome.

"Managing and controlling my thoughts was probably one of the most important things I had to do. In a way, it was like a crowd of demons I had to fight through to get to Jesus. I had to fight to hold on to my belief. My belief didn't just happen.

"Another thing that was important was to stay away from anyone who didn't have faith for healing. I didn't even tell most of the people I knew. I felt their sympathy and their unbelief would be a drain on my own faith."

A Cloud Came Into My Room and Forced Me to the Floor

Gary had determined to worship God for at least two hours at the end of each day. "It was important that I take time out from thinking about my own problems to just worship God for the greatness and glory that is His. It was intensely comforting to do this. To feel the anxiety and fear lifting as I worshiped God was nothing short of awesome."

One night he was about to put in a videotape of praise music, when he felt that he should just stand and focus on his gratitude for what God was doing for his unborn child. Gary said, "At first I was just worshiping and thanking God, as I usually did each day. Then, a presence seemed to come into the room with me. The sense of presence increased and became a crushing pressure. The weight of the pressure began to increase and forced me to the floor. I was unable to stand. I looked up, and a cloud seemed to be filling the room and blocked out the lights. At first, I felt terrified, and I tried to crawl away and out of the room. Then, I said to myself, 'You idiot! This is what you have been praying for!' The presence was God, and I knew that I had better stay put."

I Realized That the Time Had Finally Come

"The same thing happened the next night. I started to worship God, and again an overwhelming sense of pressure and of weight came upon me. This time I recalled a dream I had had some months before, in which a man brought his son to me for healing at the hospital. The boy was schizophrenic and had a brain tumor. I remembered that in the dream, I had laid my hand on the boy's head and he was instantly healed. I realized that God was prophetically telling me to go lay my hand on my baby for healing, and that the appointed time had come!"

Gary went to find Marie so he could pray for the baby. At about the same time, Gary's sister-in-law, who was 2,000 miles away, woke from sleep with a strong urge to pray for Gary and Marie. She got out of her bed at 2:00 in the morning and started praying.

Meanwhile, Marie had been stirred by an impulse to be with Gary that she couldn't explain. She was ready to get into bed and go to sleep when she just felt like she should go see

Gary. As she walked toward the room he was in for prayer, she spoke quietly to God and said, "Lord, whatever you have for me, I accept. I surrender my entire life to you. I know it will be okay." She just wanted God to help her trust Him.

A Surge of Pure Love Knocked Me to My Knees!

Gary and Marie met in the hallway of their home. Marie describes what happened next: "After a few words, Gary laid his hand on my tummy and prayed, and at first, nothing happened. Gary refused to accept this disappointment and tried to pray again, and still nothing happened. Finally on the third time, he laid his other hand on top of my head, and this time, a surge of power came out of his hands and went into the baby and me."

Gary said, "As soon as I put my hand on Marie's head, I felt a surge of pure love that physically knocked me to the ground on my knees, overwhelmingly aware of God's awesome holiness. I spoke to God and said, 'Lord, You are so infinitely and absolutely pure. I am not worthy of your presence.' I forgot about everything except this awesome presence for a long time."

Marie said, "I don't remember too much about what

happened, but I remember that when Gary touched my head, I was shot through with a profound feeling of warmth. I felt so completely loved and comforted, like nothing I had ever before experienced. The feeling of God's love for me was overwhelming. I dropped to the ground, but was not hurt at all. The next thing I knew, Gary and I were looking at each other. Then we realized that the baby was kicking and moving around, and we knew that we had our miracle. Our baby was safe."

Then we realized that the baby was kicking and moving around, and we knew that we had our miracle.

THE BIRTH OF HEALTHY BABY CAROLYN

Gary suggested getting proof with an additional ultrasound,

but Marie had had enough of ultrasounds. Marie knew that God heals gradually as well as by means of sudden miracles. If God was going to heal the baby gradually, that wouldn't show on the ultrasound. What was important to her was to believe Him. They decided to trust God to the very end, and just wait for a healthy baby to be born to them.

The testing showed no disability

of any kind.

Gary said, "The devil did not give up. Our minds continued to be attacked by doubts. This time it took the form of 'Did that really happen? Did we imagine it? Were we both hallucinating?' So we did not give up our commitment to daily speak God's promises until our perfect little daughter, Carolyn, was brought forth.

"Complete testing was performed both at the time of her

birth and some months later. The testing showed no disability of any kind."

Today, the little girl of this story is a teenager. Her name is Carolyn, and she is beautiful. She plays soccer, has a lot of friends, and is in the top 3 percent of her class at school. Gary has returned to work as a physician, and Marie has her hands full raising their family. They give their testimony gladly, and many people have been helped by hearing what God did for them because they trusted Him.

WHAT YOU CAN DO

1. Study the miracles written about in the Bible. Notice what extra thing each person did just before Jesus healed him or her.

2. Understand the difference between facts and eternal truth, and determine to trust God's Word above anything that your mind can throw at you.

3. Realize that the devil does not want you to win, and will use your mind and your weaknesses to defeat you if he can.

4. Find Scripture verses that express the need you are bringing before God.

5. Repeat God's promises to yourself many times a day. Write down important promises and meditate on them, but be sure to speak them out loud. If you know others who understand what you are doing, talk about these promises and what they mean to you.

6. Don't allow your need to become more important than your friendship with God. Make sure to take time every day to worship God, experiencing His presence as best you can. The Bible says, "Be still and know that I am God" (Ps. 46:10). He is present within you.

THE
INCOMPLETE
CHURCH

BONUS

SID ROTH

THE
INCOMPLETE
CHURCH

BRIDGING THE GAP BETWEEN GOD'S CHILDREN

5

WHEN THE PATTERN IS RIGHT...

I AM A JEW. Although as I was growing up I attended a traditional synagogue, it never dawned on me that I could know God personally. The stories about Moses, Noah, and Abraham belonged to another era. God seemed to be a million miles away—not relevant to my life. Even the most devout, older men in the synagogue were more interested in the ritualistic prayers and fellowship with their friends than in having an intimate relationship with God.

Today, most Jewish people are more secular than religious. When I was young, Jews at least went to the synagogue on high holidays like Rosh Hashanah and Yom Kippur. Now the majority of my people do not attend services at all.

When I encountered Jesus at the age of 30, everything in my world changed. I not only knew God was real, but I now knew Him personally. My biggest shock was to discover that Christians, for the most part, act like most Jews. They know about God. They believe in Him. They think they will probably go to Heaven. Yet some have greater intimacy with their denomination than with God. Others attend church merely for the social interaction. These Sunday and "high-holiday" (Easter and Christmas) Christians compartmentalize God according to their convenience. They treat Jesus more as their servant than as their Lord. They surrender Sunday mornings—not their lives.

Many churches have evolved into nothing more than religious warehouses filled with people bound for hell. Members are made to feel as if they are acceptable to God without repentance of sin. Their church experience is as spectators who never fulfill their destinies in God. Tragically, many do not even have a personal relationship with Jesus.

Over the years, I began to see that even some of the better churches are filled with religious tradition. The pastors appear to be more concerned with the offering, announcements, a full sermon, and a timely ending than with yielding to the leading of the Holy Spirit.

The more I hungered for greater intimacy with God, the more dissatisfied I became. Then God led me to study the history of the early Church. The blinders of tradition fell from my eyes. I began to see the Scriptures in a whole new light. Now I understand why there are so few miracles, even in believing, Spirit-filled churches. Now I know why so few believers fulfill their destiny in God. Now I know why the system forces the services to be man-controlled rather than God-controlled. Now I know why there is so little compassion for the souls of men and for the poor. Now I know why the sins of secular society pervade the Church. Now I know how we have grieved the Holy Spirit through ignorance, compromise, tradition, and the fear of man. Now I know why the glory under Moses was greater than our best churches today.

God has been waiting for a generation of believers to follow the cloud of His presence just as the

Israelites followed the cloud in the wilderness. The cloud is moving. Will you follow the cloud to glory, or will you remain stuck in your old ways? Only a few of the older believers will enter this new land. The rest will observe it from afar. I am hungry for more. How about you?

Just as God had a specific plan for the Israelites to enter the Promised Land, He also instructed them on how to enter His glory. God said to Moses, *"See that you make all things according to the **pattern**..."* (Heb. 8:5). The pattern is God's bridge to intimacy. When the pattern is right, the glory explodes. Notice that I did not say *formula*, but *pattern*. Man wants to place God in a box, which is why we have so many religions and denominations. God is too big to be limited by our attempts to define Him. We cannot reduce His pattern to a formula. Formulas lead us to tradition, and tradition to fossilized, dead religion. The biblical pattern always leads to greater intimacy with God.

It also leads to unity between Jew and Gentile. I believe that today God is calling us to a new level in which both Jewish and Gentile believers will come together as One New Man—yielded to His Spirit and walking in power. *"For I am about to do something new. See, I have already begun"* (Isa. 43:19 NLT).

FIRST THE NATURAL, THEN THE SPIRITUAL

God's pattern that defines the relationship between the Church and the Jewish people is explained in First Corinthians 15:46: *"The spiritual is not first, but the natural, and afterward the spiritual."* First, God acts with His natural people, Israel; then He acts with His spiritual people, the Church. His true Church is made up of those who genuinely believe in Jesus as Savior and Lord (both Jew and Gentile). The Church and Israel are *mishpochah*, which is Hebrew for "family." Whatever happens to Israel dramatically affects the restoration of the Church.

For example, in 1897 Theodor Herzl convened the first Zionist Congress in Basel, Switzerland, to investigate the formation of a Jewish homeland. The beginning of the restoration of the land birthed the beginning of the restoration of the manifest presence of the Holy Spirit in the Church. On New Year's Eve 1900, at a Bible school in Topeka, Kansas, a 30-year-old student named Agnes Ozman began to speak in tongues—the start of the Pentecostal Revival. Several days later, Charles Parham and other students also received the baptism of the Holy Spirit with the gift of speaking in tongues. After William Seymour sat under Parham's teaching, he took this fire to a home prayer meeting in Los Angeles that birthed the world-famous Azusa Street Revival.

Around the time when Israel became a nation in 1948, God responded by bringing the healing revival to the United States. Over 100 evangelists such as Oral Roberts, Kathryn Kuhlman, T.L. Osborn, and Kenneth Hagin began tremendous healing ministries. Billy Graham's ministry also started then.

In 1967, Israel regained possession of Jerusalem for the first time since the temple was destroyed. That same year, the Catholic Charismatic movement started.

It went on to impact Christians from all denominations. The late 1960s also gave birth to the Jesus Movement, which swept thousands of hippies into the Kingdom of God.

Around the time of the Yom Kippur War in 1973, revival broke out among Jewish people, resulting in the modern-day Messianic Jewish movement.

WHAT'S NEXT?

If you want to know what the next move of God will be—watch Israel. Because of sin, God scattered the Jewish people to the four corners of the earth. But in the last days He promises to restore them to Israel. (See Ezekiel 37:21.) In the Old Covenant, the nation of Israel was a divided land. The northern kingdom was called Israel, and the southern kingdom, Judah. Judah and Israel fought with each other. God promises to restore these two kingdoms and to return them to their land. They will be one nation under one King:

THE INCOMPLETE CHURCH

And I will make them one nation in the
land, on the mountains of Israel; and
one king shall be king over them all;
they shall no longer be two nations, nor
shall they ever be divided into two
kingdoms again (Ezekiel 37:22).

Today we are seeing these Scriptures fulfilled before our eyes. Israel is a nation again, and the Jews are returning to Israel in record numbers. A sign of the hastening of the prophetic time clock is when the Jews from the north of Israel (from the former Soviet Union) return to the land. Jeremiah 16:14-16 says that once this happens, Jews from the entire world will return to Israel.

We are also beginning to see the spiritual fulfillment of Ezekiel's prophecy. The two covenant peoples of God, Jews and Christians, who have been divided for centuries, will unite under one King—Jesus. This will cause a spiritual explosion in the Church. The devil's worst nightmare will come to pass when the sleeping giant, the Church, finally realizes that the underlying purpose for the current outpourings of the Holy Spirit is to equip believers with power to evangelize the Jew. When the Jewish people join with the Gentiles to form One New Man, it will trigger a major release of power to evangelize the world. But before the Church can enter this glorious future, it must first overcome its anti-Semitic past.

RESOURCES

P E G G Y   J O Y C E   R U T H

To order *Psalm 91*, contact her at 877-972-6657.

Also visit her Website:
www.peggyjoyceruth.org.

If you wish to write to

T O M   or   S I D   R E N F R O,
they can be contacted at the following address:

Thomas Renfro, MD
12200-B Carolina Road
Coeburn, VA 24230
tomr@mounet.com

SID ROTH'S
IT'S SUPERNATURAL
AND MESSIANIC VISION

P.O. Box 39222
Charlotte, NC 28278

Telephone: (704) 943-6500

Fax: (704) 943-6501

E-mail: info@sidroth.org

Visit Sid's Website:
www.SidRoth.org

Messianic Vision Canada
PO Box 5100
Markham Industrial Park
Markham, Ontario L3R054

E-mail: PartnerServices@sidroth.ca

CHECK SID'S SPEAKING ITINERARY.

Watch online or download archives of his TV show, *It's Supernatural!* and his radio show, *Messianic Vision*—or subscribe to the podcasts!

Shop an online catalog jam-packed with mentoring tools and resource materials.

Enjoy a library of articles on topics such as Jewish roots, the One New Man, Israel updates, powerful prayer, supernatural healing and experiencing the presence of God, and much, much more!

www.SidRoth.org

THEY THOUGHT FOR THEMSELVES

BY SID ROTH

The people featured in this book come from widely divergent backgrounds, including a holocaust survivor, a multimillionaire, a media executive, and a Ph.D. They range in upbringing from Atheist to Orthodox.

What is the common denominator among those in this unusual group?

They all thought for themselves, and they dared to confront the forbidden.

Believed by many to be the best book for unsaved Jewish people, it belongs in your home and church library.

ISBN: 978-0-7684-2842-1
Cost: Donation of $15.00, which includes shipping.

THE INCOMPLETE CHURCH

BY SID ROTH

This timely book explores what was stolen by the deceiver in both Judaism and Christianity and reveals what will happen when the truth in both converges.

"And wherever the double [Jew and Christian] *river shall go, every living creature which swarms shall live. And there shall be a very great number of fish* [revival]..." (Ezekiel 47:9).

What is at stake in this convergence of Jew and Gentile? The salvation of the world!

ISBN: 978-0-7684-2437-9

IN THE RIGHT HANDS, THIS BOOK WILL CHANGE LIVES!

Most of the people who need this message will not be looking for this book. To change their lives, you need to put a copy of this book in their hands.

> *But others (seeds) fell into good ground, and brought forth fruit, some a hundred-fold, some sixty-fold, some thirty-fold* (Matthew 13:8).

Our ministry is constantly seeking methods to find the good ground, the people who need this anointed message to change their lives. Will you help us reach these people?

> *Remember this—a farmer who plants only a few seeds will get a small crop. But the one who plants generously will get a generous crop* (2 Corinthians 9:6).

EXTEND THIS MINISTRY BY SOWING
3 BOOKS, 5 BOOKS, 10 BOOKS, OR MORE TODAY,
AND BECOME A LIFE CHANGER!

Thank you,

Don Nori Sr., Founder
Destiny Image
Since 1982